Srijon Chowdhury

Srijon Chowdhury
Same Old Song

Edited by Amanda Donnan

Frye Art Museum 2022

Curator's Acknowledgments

I am sincerely grateful to the many individuals and organizations who have made the exhibition *Srijon Chowdhury: Same Old Song* and this publication possible. I must begin by extending my profound gratitude to Srijon Chowdhury for his innumerable contributions as artist, co-curator, and collaborator. Working with him to conceptualize the group exhibition *Door to the Atmosphere*, which is on view alongside *Same Old Song*, opened my eyes not only to many artists with whom I was previously unacquainted, but also to expansive ways of thinking about curating. Srijon was in the meantime busy undertaking the enormous task of creating a whole new body of work for *Same Old Song*: an epic, self-cannibalizing cycle of paintings the likes of which have never been seen in contemporary art. Watching the massive, fragmented human face he described manifest one feature at a time has been truly wild and tremendously rewarding.

We were lucky to work with Srijon's top-choice contributors on this volume, Mónica Belevan and SJ Cowan, who have been such good sports writing about work before and as it emerges from the studio (or bat-infested barn). I so appreciate the insightful perspectives they have brought to Srijon's work, which beautifully realize the vision behind the FAM/books series.

I am deeply thankful for the support that the Frye Foundation and Frye Art Museum members provide the museum. I am also grateful to *The Stranger*, the media sponsor for *Same Old Song*. I thank every staff member at the Frye for their contributions to the exhibitions and publications program, as well as the board of trustees for their generosity and steadfast support of the Frye's mission. I also offer my heartfelt gratitude to Joe Rosa, former director/CEO of the Frye, for supporting this project and the book series from their inceptions.

Foxy Production in New York was vital in realizing this exhibition and publication. I am especially thankful to director Michael Gillespie for lending works, providing images, and sharing expertise, as well as the rest of the gallery staff for their support. I also thank Lara and Jeff Sanderson for so graciously lending Srijon's work *Pale Rider* to the exhibition.

My deep appreciation goes to Lucia | Marquand for their work on the publication, including intrepid staff members Leah Finger, Adrian Lucia, Meghann Ney, Julia Powers, and Kestrel Rundle. Many thanks are due to Tom Eykemans, who produced the publication's stunning design using building blocks established by Purtill Family Business for this series. I am also indebted to copy editor Kathleen Garrett for her thorough and thoughtful work.

I am grateful to the Frye's manager of exhibitions and publications, Laura Landau, for her careful shepherding of this publication; and I thank Erin Langner, exhibitions and publications coordinator, for her work sourcing the book's images and related rights.

I also thank the individuals and institutions that helped with reproduction permissions: Britt Bowen, Harvard Art Museums, Cambridge, Massachusetts; Diana Edkins, Art Resource, New York; Jonathan Hoppe, Philadelphia Museum of Art; the Huntington Art Museum, San Marino, California; the Leopold Museum, Vienna; the Musée du Louvre, Paris; the Metropolitan Museum of Art, New York; Verónica Montes, Museo Nacional del Prado, Madrid; and Tate, United Kingdom.

Finally, we acknowledge that none of what we do at the Frye Art Museum would be possible if not for the Coast Salish peoples, who have since time immemorial stewarded the lands and waters of this place we now call Seattle. We offer our gratitude and respect to their elders past and present, as well as to future generations for their continued stewardship.

AMANDA DONNAN
INTERIM CO-DIRECTOR AND CHIEF CURATOR
FRYE ART MUSEUM

Artist's Acknowledgments

I must thank my partner Anna more than anything; I couldn't have made this show without her support and her taking on the extra load with the kids. I love you Anna, nothing would be possible without you. Alan and Mondie for their barn, the lunches, watching the kids, and everything. My kids, Ava, Lili, Inez, and Kahlo. Alec for usually answering my phone calls. Broc for telling me to make things better. Jack for helping me make good stretcher bars, stretch the canvases, get my lights up in the barn, and then telling me he likes my paintings. Andreas just because. Katy also. SJ for the excellent essay. Mónica for the great phone call and excellent essay. Matt Smith for the amazing fence come to life. Antoine and Nerina for being such champions. Michael and John, for the wonderful thoughtfulness. Anat for the show that led to this. Deb for my beginning. Theo too. My mom (Colleen) and Greg. My dad (Akku) and Borna. My uncle Roger. The Oregon Arts Commission and the Ford Family Foundation for their funding. And of course, Amanda and the Frye Art Museum for this opportunity, which is a dream come true. I don't know how I got so lucky.

Srijon Chowdhury
Photo: Mario Gallucci

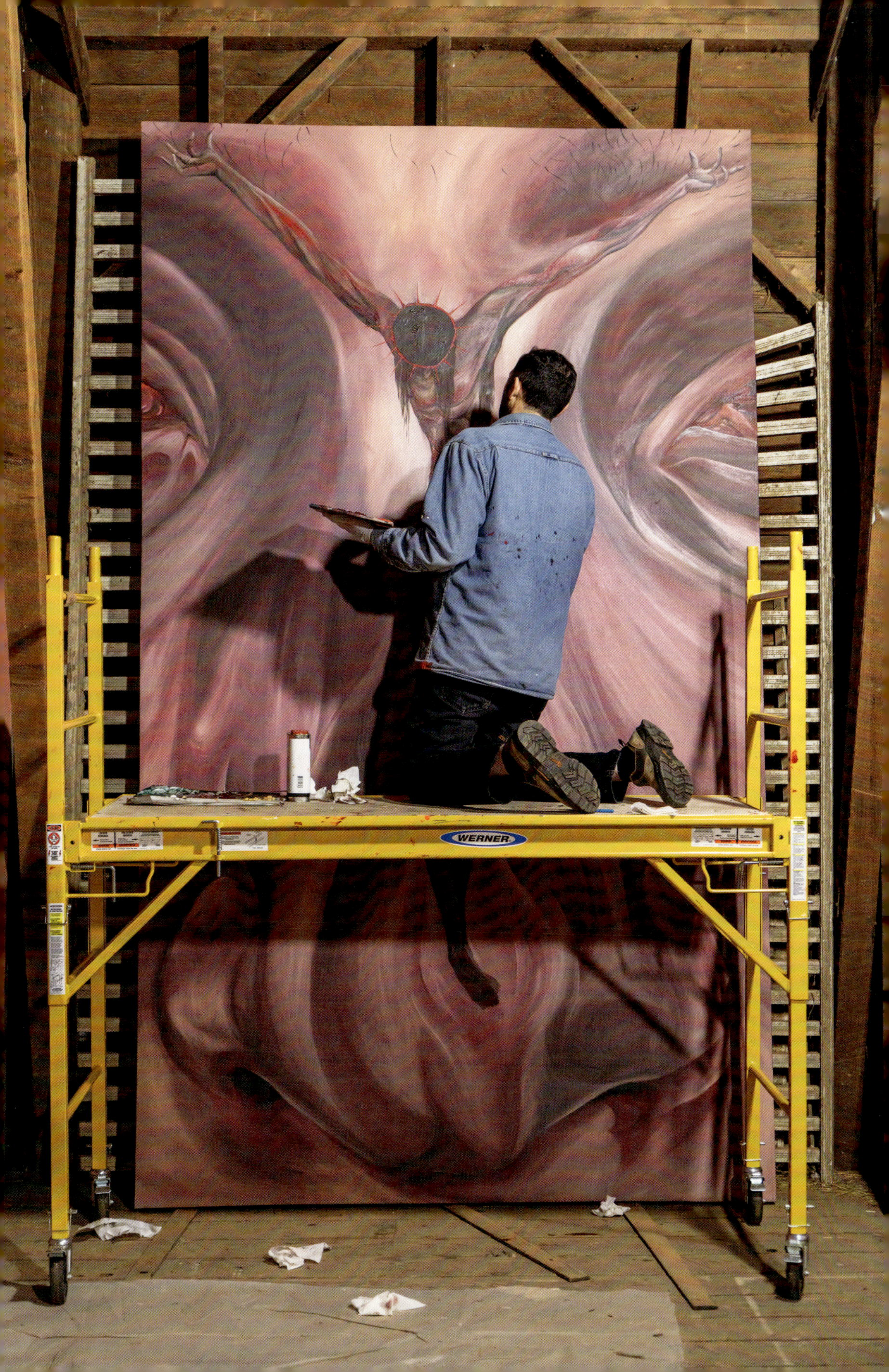
WERNER

Introduction / Doors, Portals, Passageways

Amanda Donnan

JANUARY 2022

In the perpetual uncertainty of the pandemic, some have described their experience as one of suspension, of being "frozen in amber." I may have said it myself in the early lockdown days; who can remember? That seems so long ago. Much has happened since then, and yet nothing seems to progress; there is no end in sight, and yet The End is close at hand. The cultural anthropologist Victor Turner wrote of this kind of experience—being stuck in transition or "enclosed" in the space between was and will be—as one of *liminality*.

Accordingly, I couldn't tell you exactly when Srijon Chowdhury and I started talking about the project this book accompanies—it was in the "before times." From the beginning, though, it has been imagined as a two-part artist/curator presentation of both Chowdhury's first museum solo show, *Same Old Song*, and a group exhibition entitled *Door to the Atmosphere*, co-curated by the artist and me. The latter exhibition includes works by Chowdhury's peers Sedrick Chisom, Harry Gould Harvey IV, Cindy Ji Hye Kim, Mimi Lauter, Jill Mulleady, Naudline Pierre, Eden Seifu, and TARWUK, and marks a tendency toward spirituality, myth, and the supernatural among artists working today in the United States. Apocalyptic visions, celestial visitations, and mysterious rituals and manifestations appear across the works of these artists in a diversity of mediums and styles, reflecting the wonder and the dread of living in the present as well as specters of unsettled pasts.

The exhibition title, borrowed from a work by Harry Gould Harvey IV, suggests a threshold through which one might pass from earth into ether, from the specific to the speculative, from surfaces to essences, sensations, and mood. Of course, artists have previously sought these kinds of figurative portals, especially in liminal transition periods like fin de siècle Europe, when, as Alexandra Schamel writes, "highly subjective inner worlds [were] created—aesthetic substitutes of the unpredictable world 'outside' that lies beyond comprehension."[1] All of the artists in *Door to the Atmosphere* were working in this (their) way long before COVID-19 hit pause, however;

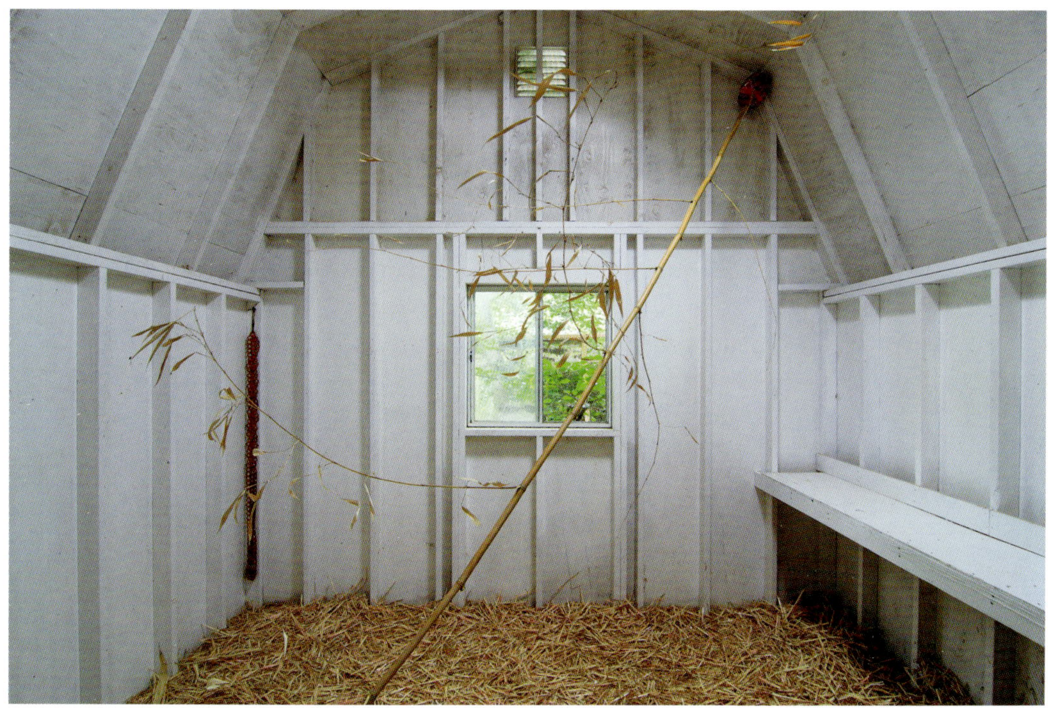

Fig. 1. Installation view of *ektor garcia and Pei-Hsuan Wang: where we meet*, curated by Haynes Riley, Chicken Coop Contemporary, Portland, OR, June 22–July 29, 2018. Courtesy of the artist. Photo: Srijon Chowdhury

we were already in a protracted phase of liminality and transition, of post-postmodernism, late capitalism, and democratic decline.

Chowdhury, for his part, has not veered off in a wholly new direction either, but has created for *Same Old Song* an ambitious suite of new works that materializes the portal or passage that Schamel suggests is the "essential motif" of the liminal imagination. While painters generally work in the second dimension and, traditionally, were concerned only with creating the illusion of space, Chowdhury here engages the third and fourth dimensions of movement through real space to evoke the inward crossing, activating metaphorical portals along the way. In the process, he constructs an interiorized sublime with all the irreducible duality of awe and terror, beauty and menace that the Romantics saw outside.

Chowdhury has been thinking spatially for some time, both within his own art practice and through the process of organizing exhibitions. In 2016, he and his wife, Anna Margaret, established a gallery on their property outside Portland, Oregon—in a large shed adjacent to another that Chowdhury uses as a studio—called Chicken Coop Contemporary (fig. 1). There they have exhibited works by artists such as Katelyn Eichwald, ektor garcia, Andreas

Gurewich, Jon Haddock, Harry Gould Harvey IV, Renée Petropoulos, Jesse Stecklow, Pei-Hsuan Wang, and Keith J. Varadi, among others; they have also hosted guest-curated projects and performances. The space is actively occupied by hens, the floor usually covered in hay: an unusual context for art objects even by the standards of Portland's garage-gallery scene, and one that the artists have often directly engaged. Stecklow, for instance, created an installation called *Collection Sites* that considered the chickens as the primary audience (figs. 2, 3).

Looking at Chowdhury's own otherworldly paintings, you might never guess he works in a barn, interrupted by scavenging pigs, chickens, and toddlers, and very much in the stream of earthy, everyday goings-on. Elements of this environment frequently appear in Chowdhury's paintings, especially Anna and their children, but therein they take on a dreamlike, archetypal quality of being both themselves and more universal representations. Much of art and storytelling can be said to function this way, through an alchemical process of transmuting individual identity into something transcendent, thereby opening portals into other subjectivities. But Chowdhury is particularly concerned with considering the present moment as part of a larger mythology and the potential of art objects—as condensations of desire and mediums of communion—to soften the boundaries around the Self. He describes himself as a "late symbolist," embracing the imminent epochal change that term implies.

The artist speaks not only of wanting to elicit a reaction from viewers, but of provoking transformation—of *transporting* them on a visceral and emotional level. One way he has endeavored to do this is by making architecturally scaled, immersive works that he sees as "backdrops to an origin story" of which the viewer is part. The titles of these installations—as in *The Garden* (2014;

Figs. 2, 3. Installation views of *Jesse Stecklow: Collection Sites*, Chicken Coop Contemporary, Portland, OR, July 22–August 30, 2017. Courtesy of the artist. Photos: Jesse Stecklow

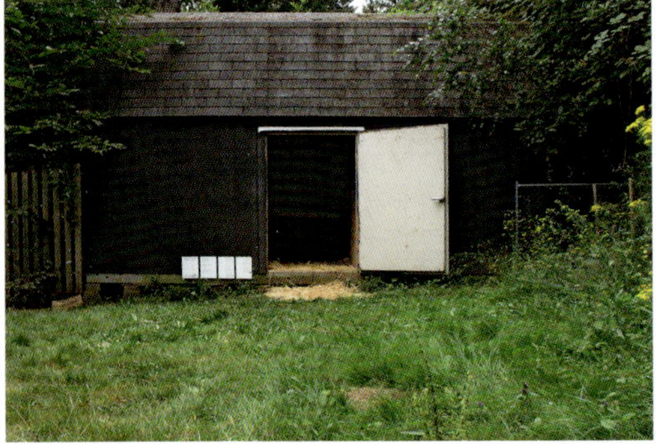

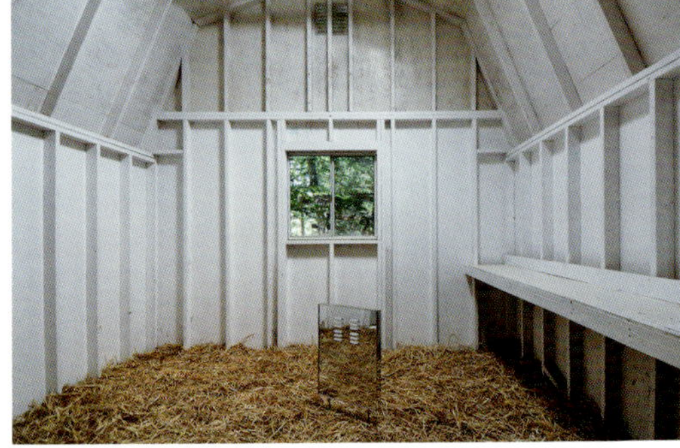

pp. 36–37) and *Revelation Theater* (2018; pp. 42–45)—frequently reinforce a connection to biblical narratives. Meanwhile, motifs like the engulfing floral pattern in works such as *Pale Rider* (2019; pp. 56–57) recall medieval allegories such as the *Unicorn Tapestries* (fig. 4), that open portals in time to ancient, legendary imaginaries.

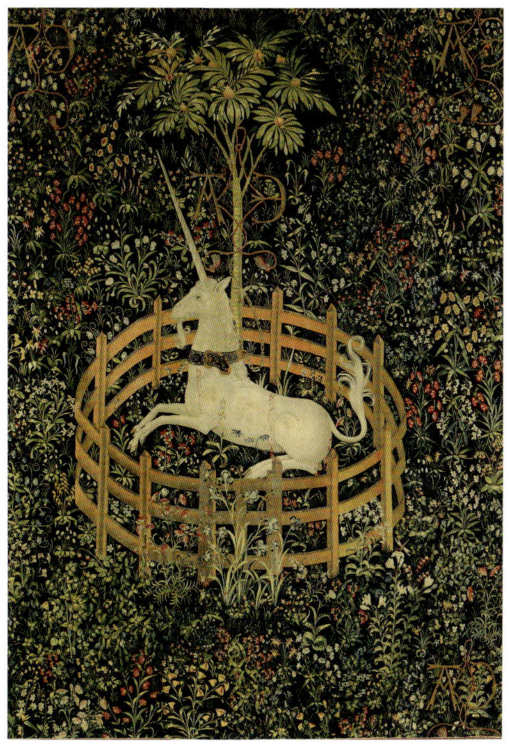

Fig. 4. *The Unicorn Rests in a Garden* (from the *Unicorn Tapestries*), 1495–1505. Wool warp with wool, silk, silver, and gilt wefts. 144⅞ × 99 in. The Metropolitan Museum of Art, Gift of John D. Rockefeller Jr., 1937, 37.80.6

Chowdhury's more intimately scaled pieces—usually twists on traditional genres like portraiture and the *vanitas* still life—also emit a potent charge, with saturated colors, deep shadows, and an eerie phosphorescence suggestive of an arcane, supernatural significance. He often references the chakras when speaking about his color choices, especially in relation to the crimson red that recurs like a leitmotif across his practice. In Tantric philosophy and meditation, crimson is the color of the root chakra, which is located at the base of the spine and is associated with grounding or stabilizing energy. For Chowdhury, red is an anchor to this body, this reality, and the beauty of simply being alive despite all that is wrong in the world. But the color has an intensifying effect, too, often declaring that this world is, in fact, *on fire*.

With *Same Old Song*, Chowdhury pursues an apotheosis of sorts in both subject matter and intended effect. The main gallery contains six enormous new paintings, each of which centers on one sensory organ of the human (inter)face: eyes, ears, nose, and a mouth that is thirty feet long (2022; pp. 76–82). The central facial feature in each piece acts as a framing device for or composite of smaller images, many of which are sampled from Chowdhury's previous paintings to convene a retrospective by other means. Though the facial features are modeled on Chowdhury's and Anna's attributes, this may be seen as an invitation into the artist's head and a theatricalization of the imperfect communication process by which an artist encodes meanings for the viewer to interpret. Though these messages may be understood differently by each person, they most importantly signify the effort to bridge individual consciousness and achieve intersubjectivity, maybe even realize interdependency. The notion of a common fate is found within the paintings themselves,

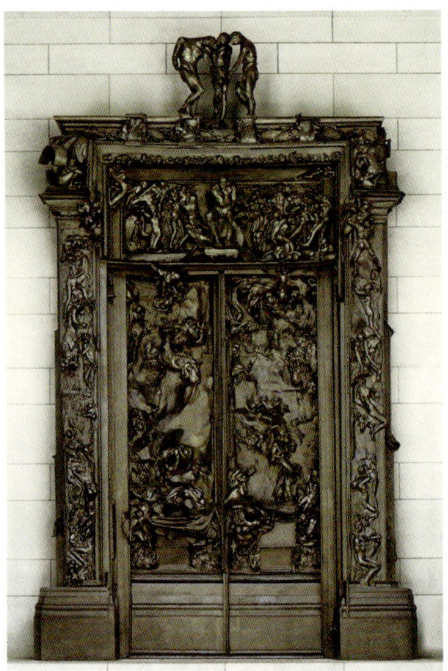

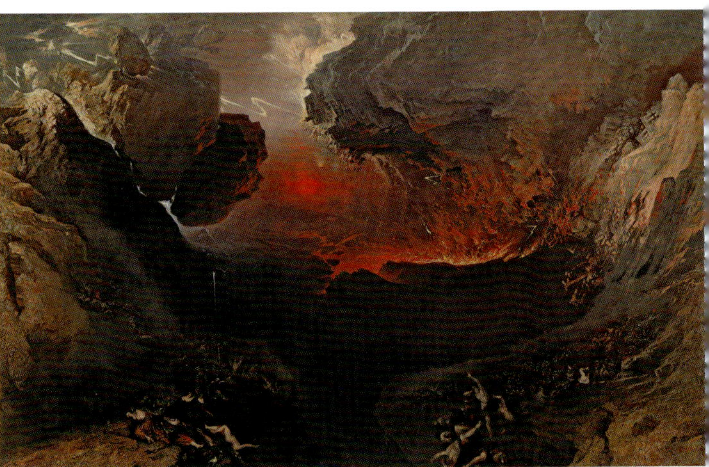

Fig. 5. Auguste Rodin. *The Gates of Hell*, modeled 1880–1917; cast 1926–28. Bronze. 20 ft. 10¾ × 158 × 33⅜ in. Philadelphia Museum of Art, Bequest of Jules E. Mastbaum, 1929, F1929-7-128

Fig. 6. John Martin. *The Great Day of His Wrath* from the *Judgement Series*, 1851–53. Oil paint on canvas. 77⅖ × 119 in. Tate, N05613. Photo: Tate

for instance, in the inferno framed by parted (and *seething*) lips in *Mouth (Divine Dance)* (2022; pp. 76–77). When making this work, Chowdhury was thinking of Auguste Rodin's *Gates of Hell* (fig. 5), in which writhing figures representing the whole of humanity emerge from and are subsumed by the same inchoate fluid mass. As in Chowdhury's installation, Rodin's massive gates include images that recur elsewhere in his oeuvre, like the archetypal philosopher *The Thinker* (1904) and the lovers in *The Kiss* (1901–04).

The immersive scale and totalizing impetus of Chowdhury's gallery-as-human-head recalls a genealogy of pre-cinematic technologies like the panorama, as well as the apocalyptic sublime of Romantic works such as John Martin's *Judgement Series* (fig. 6). His is a drama of interiority, however; the viewer surveys internalized perceptions rather than looking out over a vast exterior landscape. An earlier analogue for Chowdhury's architectural program of paintings, cited by the artist himself, illuminates his concept further: Giulio Camillo's "Memory Theater," a sixteenth-century wooden construction modeled on the ancient Greek *ars memoria*. Classically, the "art of memory" was a memorization technique in which the main points of a speech were recalled through visualizing a sequence of symbolic objects encountered within the rooms of a building. In the Renaissance occult philosophy of Camillo's time, however, what had been a pragmatic system of attaching abstract ideas to concrete images took on magical properties. Using the "eye of the imagination," not only texts "but the whole cosmos could be 'memorized' and by this act magically incorporated into the human organism."[2]

Camillo endeavored to physicalize this method of comprehending the divine, creating a "built mind or soul" in the form of a seven-tiered auditorium structure for one or two observers that encapsulated the entirety of the universal order. On each level, he fastened "actual carved images of the archetypes behind reality (represented mostly by planetary gods) . . . with masses of written material stored in drawers" under each.[3] Chowdhury directly referenced this precedent in his installation *Memory Theater* (fig. 7), placing sculptures created by other artists around the outside of a circular scrim structure so they appeared as silhouettes, "outside of time," to viewers inside. In *Same Old Song*, his spatialized portrait-cum-memory theater again presents a subjective microcosm of meaningful symbols rather than *the* universal order, but Camillo's enduring influence positions his work in relation to a lineage of practices oriented more toward the sacred than the spectacular.

Indeed, Chowdhury has created a whole liturgical program, a processional portal-pathway into "the head" in which significant forms and personages are invoked and, in some cases, reprised as in incantation. In the first gallery, the viewer encounters a number of small paintings along with *Pale Rider* (2019, pp. 56–57)—the

Fig. 7. Installation view of *Srijon Chowdhury: Memory Theater*, Upfor, Portland, OR, April 13–May 28, 2016. Photo: Mario Gallucci

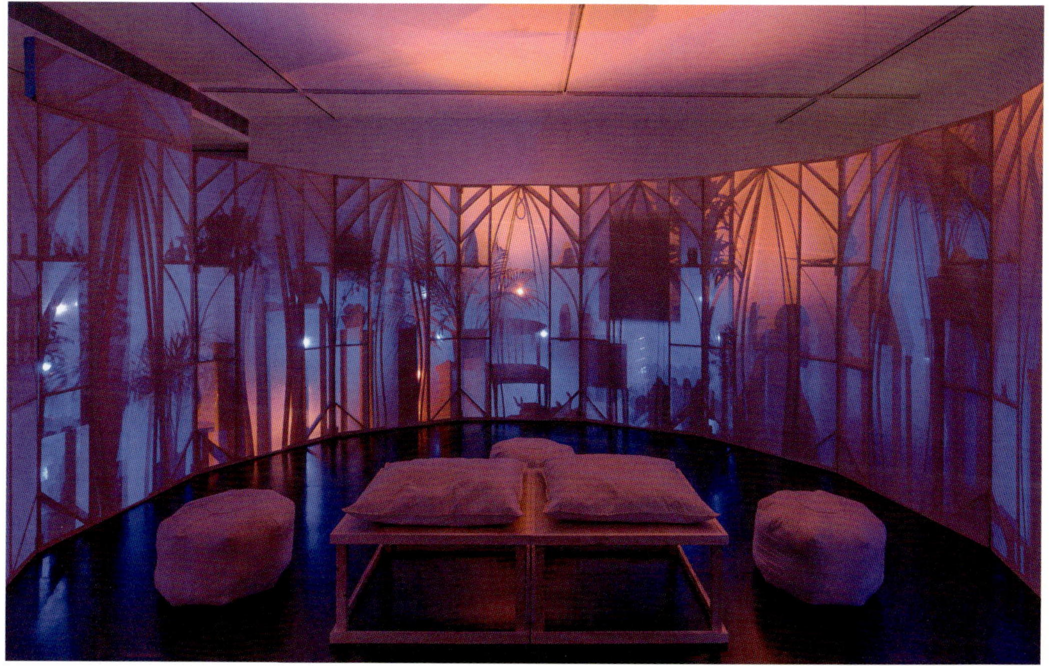

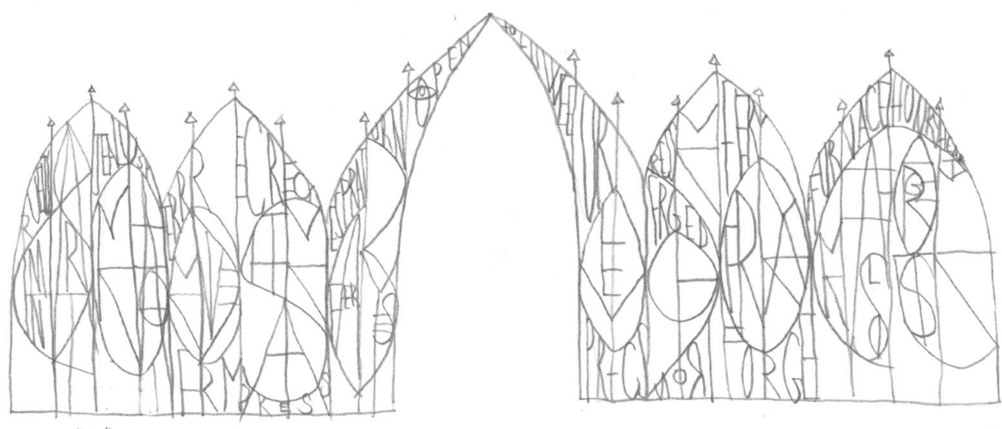

Fig. 8. Chowdhury's sketch of *Sigil Gate*, 2022

sixteen-foot-long painting in which the fertile whimsy of the *Unicorn Tapestries* meets the Book of Revelation in the guise of a ghostly horsewoman of the apocalypse. Holding a scythe, she gallops past a stylized fence composed of script that, though difficult to discern, is in fact the text of William Blake's poem *A Divine Image*:

> Cruelty has a Human Heart
> And Jealousy a Human Face
> Terror the Human Form Divine
> And Secrecy, the Human Dress
>
> The Human Dress, is forged Iron
> The Human Form, a fiery Forge.
> The Human Face, a Furnace seal'd
> The Human Heart, its hungry Gorge.

Chowdhury describes the fence as separating the viewer from the field of flowers and the promise they represent: "Flowers, nature, will always come back, no matter what happens," he says.[4] Beautiful but ephemeral, associated with spring and birth as well as death, flowers are microcosms of the sublime.

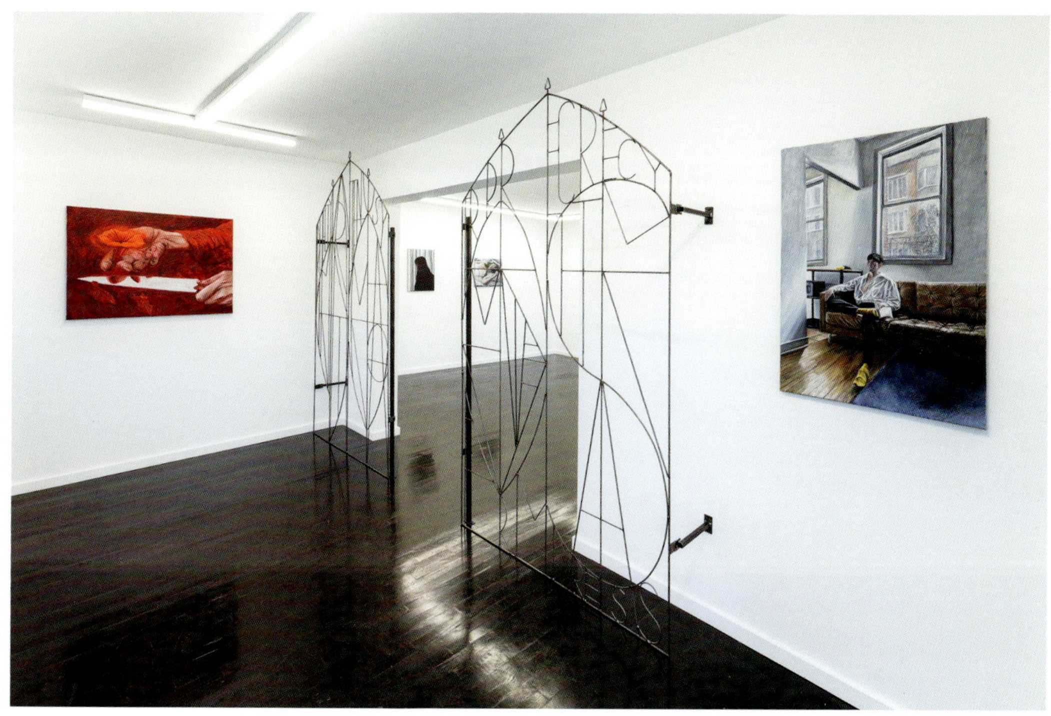

Fig. 9. Srijon Chowdhury. *Sigil Gate*, 2022. Welded steel. Two panels, 90 × 55 in. each. Installation view, *Srijon Chowdhury: Groundhog Day*, SE Cooper Contemporary, Portland, OR. Photo: Mario Gallucci

In the next gallery, visitors find that the represented fence has materialized in real space, and they must pass through it to enter the large gallery beyond. The wrought-iron structure repeats *A Divine Image* but includes original text as well: a protection spell that reads "Desperate fear burns eyes open / Our love protects" has been inserted in the center to form open gateway doors (figs. 8, 9). Chowdhury designed the fence, in both *Pale Rider* and its physical manifestation, as a sigilization of the given text. Descended from the Middle Ages and adapted in the twentieth century by occultists like Austin Osman Spare, sigils are pictograms or glyphs that represent the maker's desired outcome and are "charged" by force of that person's will. In medieval times, specific sigils were used to summon a corresponding angel or demon, but modern sigils most often take the form of text describing the maker's wish condensed into a monogram, as in Chowdhury's gate. Blake's poem and the artist's invocation are not (at least, easily) legible, but that isn't necessary for them to work.

The double invocation of Blake is in and of itself significant, and not only as a herald of the apocalyptic sublime. Blake was a visionary iconoclast who, in elaborating the Bible and his own mythological world, articulated the union of good and evil while condemning orthodoxies like organized religion, class and gender inequality, and stultifying social strictures around sex. Included in the collection of poems *Songs of Experience* in 1804 (fig. 10), *A Divine Image* is in fact a pendant to the poem *The Divine Image*, which appeared in *Songs of Innocence* and describes in similar structure the mercy, pity, peace, and love that are the divine virtues attributed to God. In Blake's view, man (*sic*) is made in God's image as much as God is made in man's image, so the evil aspects of humanity depicted in *A Divine Image* are also qualities of the divine. This is encapsulated in his notion of the "marriage of heaven and hell."

Blake's art and attitude have long exerted an influence on Chowdhury and on several of the artists in *Door to the Atmosphere* as well. Harvey describes Blake in apropos terms as a progenitor of proletarian faith who articulated belief outside of dogmatic religious structures to reveal "the heaven you can build in your head."[5] Chowdhury, however, beyond quoting Blake's influences, here condenses *A Divine Image* into an amulet, a physicalized emblem of the cruelty, jealousy, terror, and secrecy described therein. It might seem counterintuitive to summon these forces in the form of a sigil, but the artist views the poem as being about "naming evil" and, in doing so, "taking its power away."

> The sigil's magic is partly about neutralizing the power of evil. The activation of our love in the central gateway is a protection spell, keeping those negative forces at bay. When I think of what evil means now, it's essentially the suicidal greed for power that is destroying our planet and society. I usually try not to think about it, which is another kind of evil, I guess. The line "desperate fear burns our eyes open" is maybe for me—a wish to interrupt my nihilistic tendencies.[6]

Inaccessible behind the fence structure, Chowdhury has included another multivalent symbol of humanity's dark side from the Frye Art Museum's collection: Franz von Stuck's painting *Die Sünde* (Sin) (fig. 11). One of several nearly identical versions of

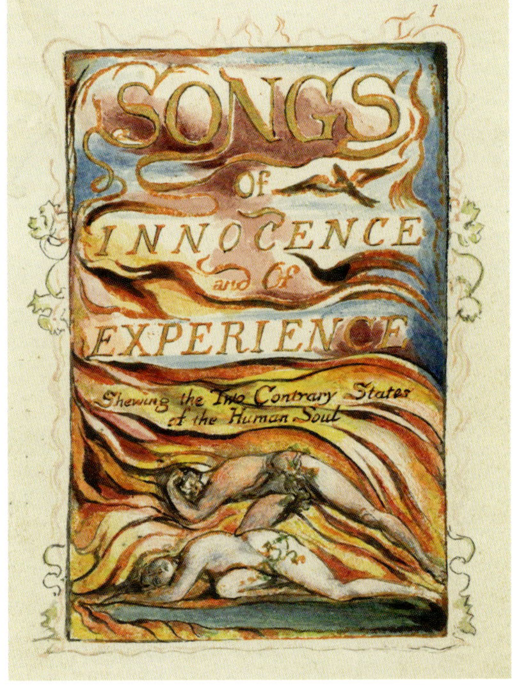

Fig. 10. William Blake. *Songs of Innocence and of Experience, Shewing the Two Contrary States of the Human Soul*: combined title page, ca. 1825. Relief etching printed in orange-brown ink and hand-colored with watercolor and gold. Sheet: 6 3/16 × 5 9/16 in. The Metropolitan Museum of Art, Rogers Fund, 1917, 17.10.1

a work first exhibited in 1893 and called an "icon of fin de siècle Munich," Stuck's *Sin* blends eroticism and religious subject matter: the biblical figure of Eve with an archetypal femme fatale. That this figure may also have been intended to evoke Gustave Flaubert's then-popular orientalist seductress Salammbô—who dances naked with a "holy" python from the temple of Eschmoûn—is supported by the painting's artist-made frame, which takes the form of a gilded temple front. One of the *Sin* paintings hung in a custom-built altar in the artist's lavish home, Villa Stuck; the image was clearly one of exalted and dangerous Dionysian allure.

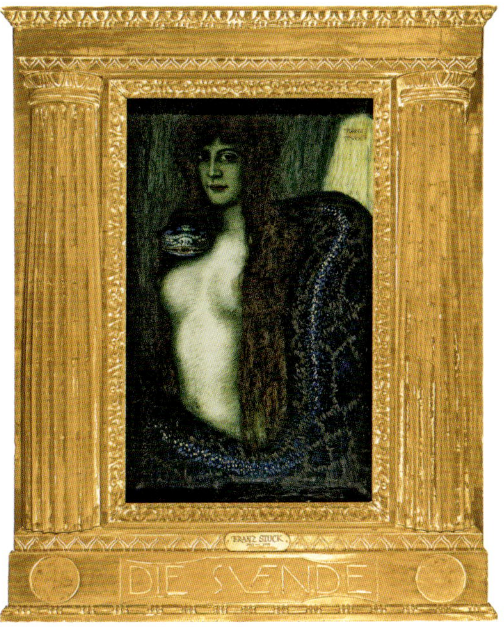

Fig. 11. Franz von Stuck. *Die Sünde* (Sin), ca. 1908. Tempera on canvas. 34⅞ × 21⅝ in. Frye Art Museum, Founding Collection, Gift of Charles and Emma Frye, 1952.169. Photo: Spike Mafford

Like Blake, Stuck embraced the contradictions and moral ambiguities of the human condition, creating a "programmatic manifesto for an era distinguished by . . . epochal disjuncture" and reinscribing modern life within transhistorical mythic traditions.[7] Including these references along the passageway into the interiorized sublime of his contemporary headspace, Chowdhury signposts a lineage of artistic forebears who expressed the inexorable duality of experience. In the essays that follow, Mónica Belevan and SJ Cowan open portals to other art historical resonances—as elemental as prehistoric cave painting and as excessive as the Late Baroque. While to some extent their texts approach Chowdhury's work from opposite sides—life and death, love and dread, the sensual and the spiritual—both traverse the knotted core in which these forces are found to be intertwined. Enclosed within transition, the liminal imagination builds passages that ultimately lead in circles.

The Family Romance of Srijon Chowdhury

Mónica Belevan

The first time I made direct contact with Srijon Chowdhury was on December 16, 2021, the fiftieth anniversary of the day on which the country now known as Bangladesh secured its independence from West Pakistan with the largest surrender of soldiers since World War II. Our conversation thus began on a note that has defined my recent exchanges with millennial painters of East Asian descent: the personal is the political, if in sometimes unexpected ways. The expediting synchronicity that provided me with the frame for this written portrait was that our painter's father is Akku Chowdhury—the founder of the Liberation War Museum in Dhaka, and a former freedom fighter. It is also an unusual note on which to open an essay on Chowdhury, who is in no way an *overtly* political painter—but that's the point precisely. I intend to write this essay sideways, as he might have painted it.

Chowdhury's style is moody, prismatic, and viscous. An examination of his work points toward a crystallization process in two stages over several years. The first of these, a kind of nucleation, involves a series of localized phase transitions that can be followed as developing motifs throughout his work: juxtapositions of diverse opacity and hardness, a staccato or will-o'-the-wisp use of color, the sense of currents jetting underneath an ice sheet, an amalgam of fabric, ectoplasm, tissue.

The earliest art featured on his Instagram account is almost blurred, draft-y even; the figures faceless, phantasmatic, and inchoate. As the timeline progresses, these forms begin to build up sediment, gaining assertiveness and definition. The linework becomes more precise, a themescape and manner begin to congeal, the first folds appear. There is a thickening in style and substance as if seen through glass—a liquid solid or a solid liquid—and, comparably to how glass cracks not on account of extreme temperatures, but because of the rate of *change* in temperature, Chowdhury's painting has become increasingly sophisticated as the demands on his craft have intensified.

While a hieratic distancing effect—a sense of mediacy and material tension—is distinctive to Chowdhury's work throughout, time observably bestows it with a growing sense of structure. This paradoxical plasticity is also what is most difficult to pin down in Chowdhury's art because it is uniquely his, and utterly hermetic. It is most perceptible in recent fare like *The Writer* (2021; p. 74) (a portrait of Dean Kissick and his couch) and *The Comedian* (2021; p. 75), with its flaccid penis, reptile linen, and strategic, Franz von Stuck–esque cover of darkness. Chowdhury made two studies of the penis in this painting that serve as a compressed demonstration of his crystallization process. The first is fine and luminous as cat hair, a diaphanous dishcloth (fig. 1). The second pass, which introduces detailing through contrast, is a concrete and ornate architecture of the male reproductive apparatus: a veiny dueling glove or half-cocked pistol (fig. 2).

The early work is intriguingly hybrid, with light sculptures, backlit screens, and patterning that is at once evocative of batik and stained glass (figs. 3–5). There is an almost Gothic architectural component to it, a push to be structurally self-supporting whilst communicating lightness that reiterates itself in countless ways across Chowdhury's oeuvre. But there is always that primordial tension between rigidity and dynamism, where the art is captured in the physical transition from one state to another. Like plasma, it is both the most abundant phase of ordinary matter and the stuff that stars are made of. Chowdhury focuses everyday subjects in extraordinary ways.

Fig. 1. Srijon Chowdhury. *The Comedian* in progress (detail), 2021. Oil on linen. 24 × 36 in. Private collection. Photo: Srijon Chowdhury

Fig. 2. Srijon Chowdhury. *The Comedian* in progress (detail), 2021. Oil on linen. 24 × 36 in. Private collection. Photo: Srijon Chowdhury

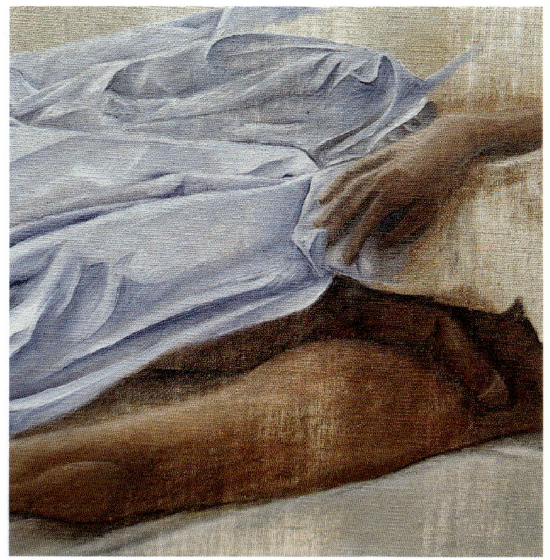

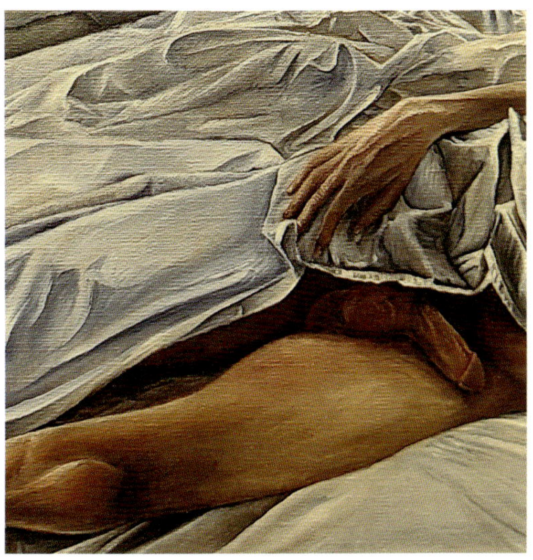

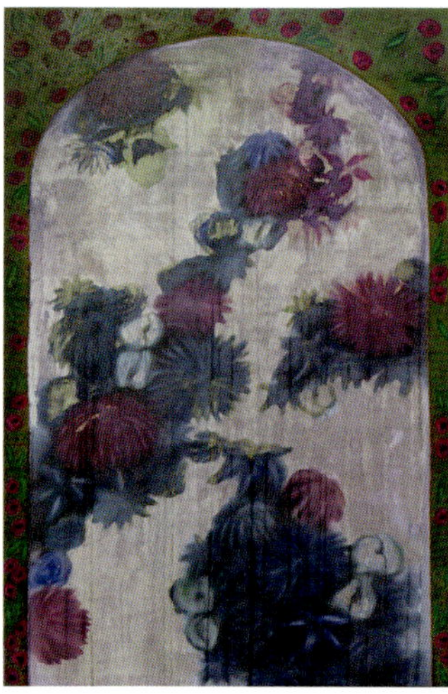

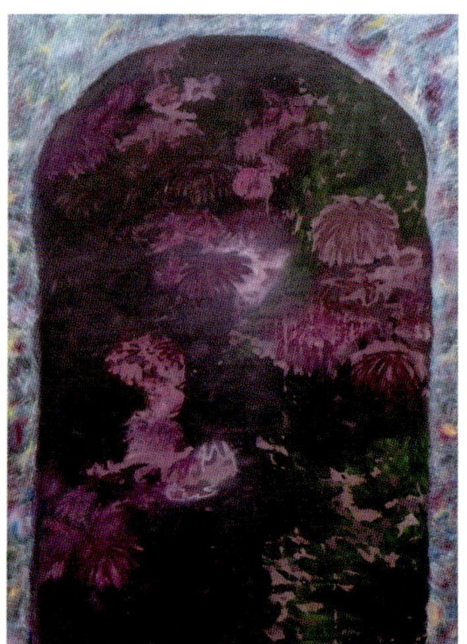

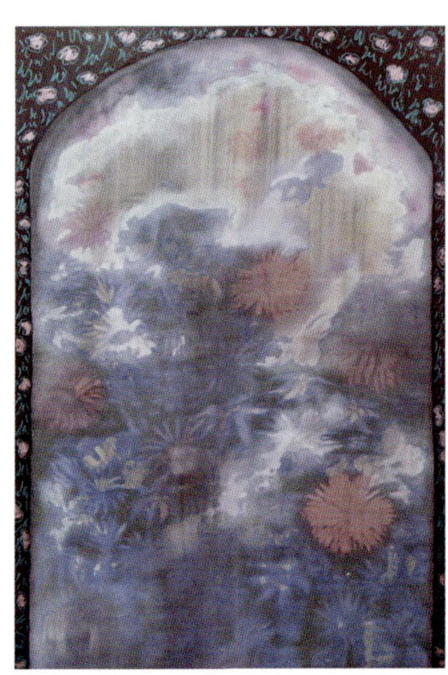

From left:

Fig. 3. Srijon Chowdhury. *Arch (green)*, 2015. Oil on linen. 72 × 48 in. Courtesy of the artist. Photo: Chris Adler

Fig. 4. Srijon Chowdhury. *Arch (white)*, 2015. Oil on linen. 72 × 48 in. Courtesy of the artist. Photo: Chris Adler

Fig. 5. Srijon Chowdhury. *Arch (blue)*, 2015. Oil on linen. 72 × 48 in. Courtesy of the artist. Photo: Chris Adler

Such complexity is not, alas, especially conducive to conversation. Chowdhury does not find it easy to talk about his work—nor, frankly, should he—so we spent some time nudging and leading our chat down a path that could coagulate into a wieldy description of this thing he does, and how it works.

He is a man of few words: "Nobody understands anyone," he tells me. He has reason enough to be wary of language, as well. Even before the Liberation War, Bangladesh had a language movement that pushed for the adoption of Bangla over Urdu. Chowdhury's grandmother was a student leader of this movement, and his father—who is from Chittagong—didn't learn Bangla until he was older. As a result of this, he was twice captured—and twice a candidate for execution—by his own army, which assumed he was a Pakistani spy because he spoke Chatgaiya. There is a very real sense in which language is fundamentally the constant realignment of misunderstandings. Art is, perhaps, more forgiving and flexible.

Though Chowdhury is not sure why we—not him and me, but everyone in general—talk so much, he reminds me we have *certainly* been painting, *and painting well*, since a rosy-fingered early human impressed the life-size image of a warty pig in a Sulawesian cave at least 45,500 years ago. Oral history has always moved from mouth to mouth, like secrets and gossip; burials were conducted earlier, but painting was among the first intentional activities that Paleolithic primitives designed against time. That the purpose of cave art was probably somewhere between the didactic and the ceremonial only stresses the degree to which painting may have marked our first, species-specific contact with the instinct we now re-cognize as art.

The fundamental mystery of cave painting is darkness—art originates in shadow and in the relative inaccessibility of yawning depths and scabrous heights. Chowdhury is unusually at ease with the dark; he has an excellent and very personal command of it. He could have easily been the sort to partake in early cave painting, as hinted by his subtly kinetic still lifes. Though he has been compared to Symbolists like Odilon Redon, I find Chowdhury rather more straightforward. He is a cineaste of sorts—like cavemen were—and so the overlap with Redon is less in the oneiric colorwork than in the *noirs*.

Chowdhury's blacks are notable. In *Blue Still Life* (fig. 6), the bottom of the plant inside the vase is patently naturalistic. As the eye shoots up the stem, however, it transitions into something very different: a *shodo* version of itself, completely stylized, crowned with an inkblot for a flower. The effect is no less disconcerting than it is effective. As far as I am concerned, this is Surrealism. A companion piece in red, *Winter Still Life* (2021; p. 70), unflattens the vase in the picture by casting an equally flat *cutout* of a shadow against the wall. The stem is almost a nerve, something out of Santiago Ramón y Cajal, that crests in a bloom resembling nothing so much as the radiant severed head of John the Baptist in Gustave Moreau's *L'Apparition* (The Apparition) (fig. 7). The candle anchoring the composition to the table also insinuates the flower as a possible projection of the flame. It is platonically Freudian.

Fig. 6. Srijon Chowdhury. *Blue Still Life*, 2021. Oil on linen. 12 × 9 in. Private collection. Photo: Charles Benton

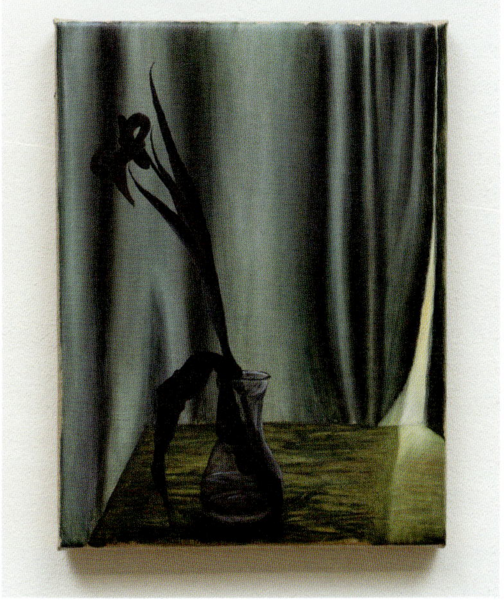

This uncanniness is the preserve of some of Chowdhury's best work: his morbid streak unforced and exquisite. It's worth remembering that, on his American mother's side, Chowdhury is the great-great-grandson of a member of the lynch party that murdered the Mormon prophet Joseph Smith, one of 200 faces of a hive mind war-painted with black gunpowder. This ferociousness, which comes to him from both sides of the family, is restrained but always latent in his output. Some of his early efforts are vaguely, disquietingly evocative of Egon Schiele's *Dead Mother* series (figs. 8, 9). Here and there, a flayed body, a demon, something resembling a *penanggalan* appears. He dedicates two paintings to the dead Ophelia: one, of her hand, pruned by hours of soaking, does such an admirable job with the skin that it seems almost ready to peel (fig. 10). The other gives the slight impression of being undead, or in the process of getting there (2018; p. 46). Ophelia locks eyes with the viewer in a sensuous and accusatory glare that undermines her usual characterization as a victim by suggesting her potential as a vampire—Hamlet's narcissistic pair.

I would have liked to interview Chowdhury in person because I suspect he says more with his hands and his face than with words. At one point we discuss the role of the body and movement in space while in the act of painting, the role of muscle memory in retreading shapes, and it is obvious that Chowdhury is what I describe as a somatic painter. He paints rapidly and with violent vigor, following long, ruminative gestations. He is a painter prone to pregnant states, and it sits well with him. He does not like to draw—which is a way of thinking and, sometimes, of overthinking—and would much rather attack the canvas with less interference. He pre-composes through a mixed approach of sketches, photos, and collages that is essentially the ur-superposition upon which he layers all his others.

He is painting his new work in his father-in-law's barn, which is not just enormous, but somewhat exposed to the Portland weather (fig. 11). I ask him if he's planning on pulling a Whistler and exposing his painting to the elements. Not quite, he says, but a little. Bat shit, Chowdhury tells me, is piled and plastered everywhere, which is just as well, as this is, indeed, a batshit project.

Up until some hours ago—the last day of my writing window—I had not seen a jot of Chowdhury's new work, as it did not exist. (Note: this is a perfectly acceptable way to write about painting). We

From left:

Fig. 7. Gustave Moreau. *L'Apparition* (The Apparition), 1876–77. Oil on canvas. 22 × 18⅜ in. Harvard Art Museums/ Fogg Museum, Bequest of Grenville L. Winthrop, 1943.268. Photo: © President and Fellows of Harvard College

Fig. 8. Srijon Chowdhury. *Revelation Theater (Fool)* (detail), 2017. Oil on linen. 126 × 72 in. Courtesy of Ciaccia Levi, Paris-Milan. Photo: Mario Gallucci

Fig. 9. Egon Schiele. *Tote Mutter (I)* (Dead Mother [I]), 1910. Oil on wood, 12⅗ × 10⁹⁄₁₀ in. Museum Leopold, Vienna, LM 475. Photo: Erich Lessing / Art Resource, NY

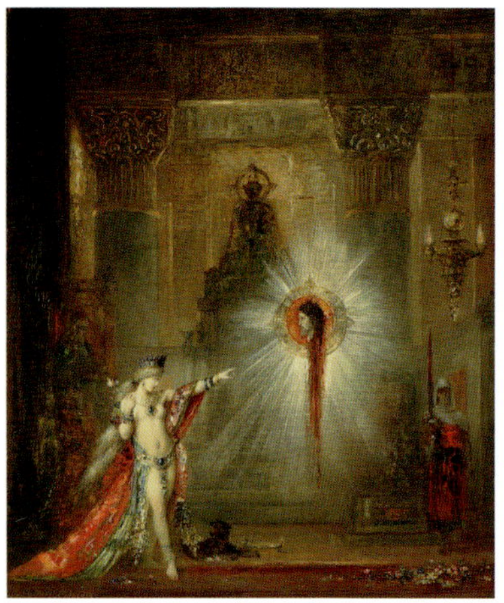

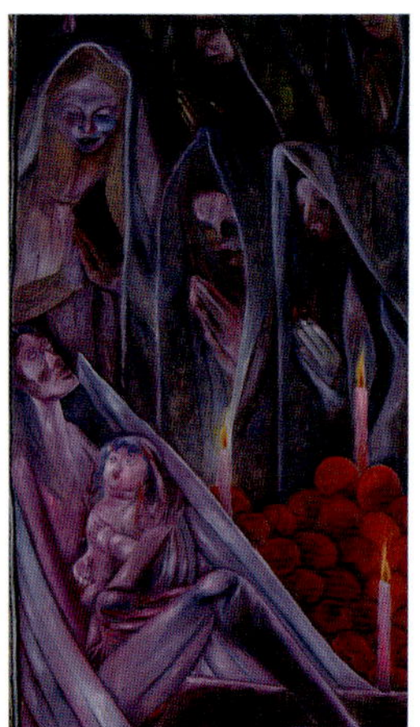

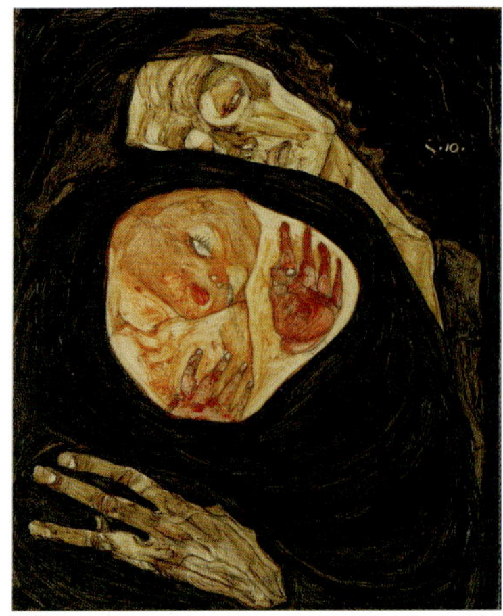

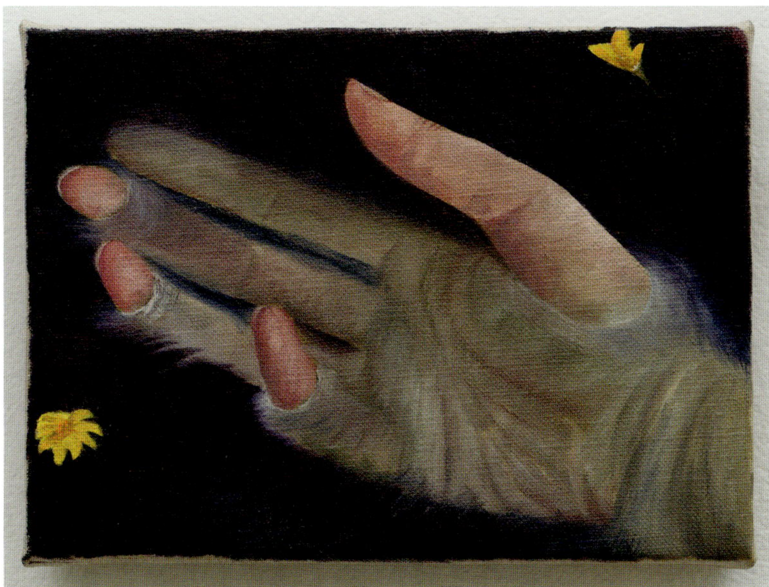

Fig. 10. Srijon Chowdhury. *Ophelia*, 2019. Oil on linen. 6 × 8 in. Private collection. Photo: Michael Underwood

had spoken about it. He had described it to me in detail, and I had tentatively sketched my understanding of it on a hospital notepad or napkin, with the intermittent ink of a hospital pen. Today, shortly before closing hours, I saw at least the early seams—the commissures of two gigantic lips—of what will soon be something to behold (2022; pp. 76–77).

Chowdhury's exhibition for the Frye Art Museum consists of six new paintings: the massive mouth I've hinted at above, at an immodest 10½ by 30 feet, engulfed in fiery, dancing figures; plus five ancillary paintings, 10½ by 6 feet each, comprising two eyes—one of them giving birth, a mythic trope I cannot say I have encountered anywhere before—plus two ears and a nose (2022; pp. 78–82). The face will be arrayed in the confines of a rectangular room—facing itself, as it were. Each and all of these paintings, together, will make use of Chowdhury's established pictorial language in some way: the big mouth, for example, is—though it is also *more than*—an extension of his large-scale inquiries; the palette will be minimal, though spiked with his signature reds; the compositions will present familiar tropes, set forth in new, adventurous, and possibly unpleasant ways.

There is a sense in which this installation—for that is how this work will be experienced, as a full-body hit—is, in the strictest, most literal sense, a meta-self-retrospective. And any retrospective, no matter how meta, presupposes a *body* of work. I have seen that work

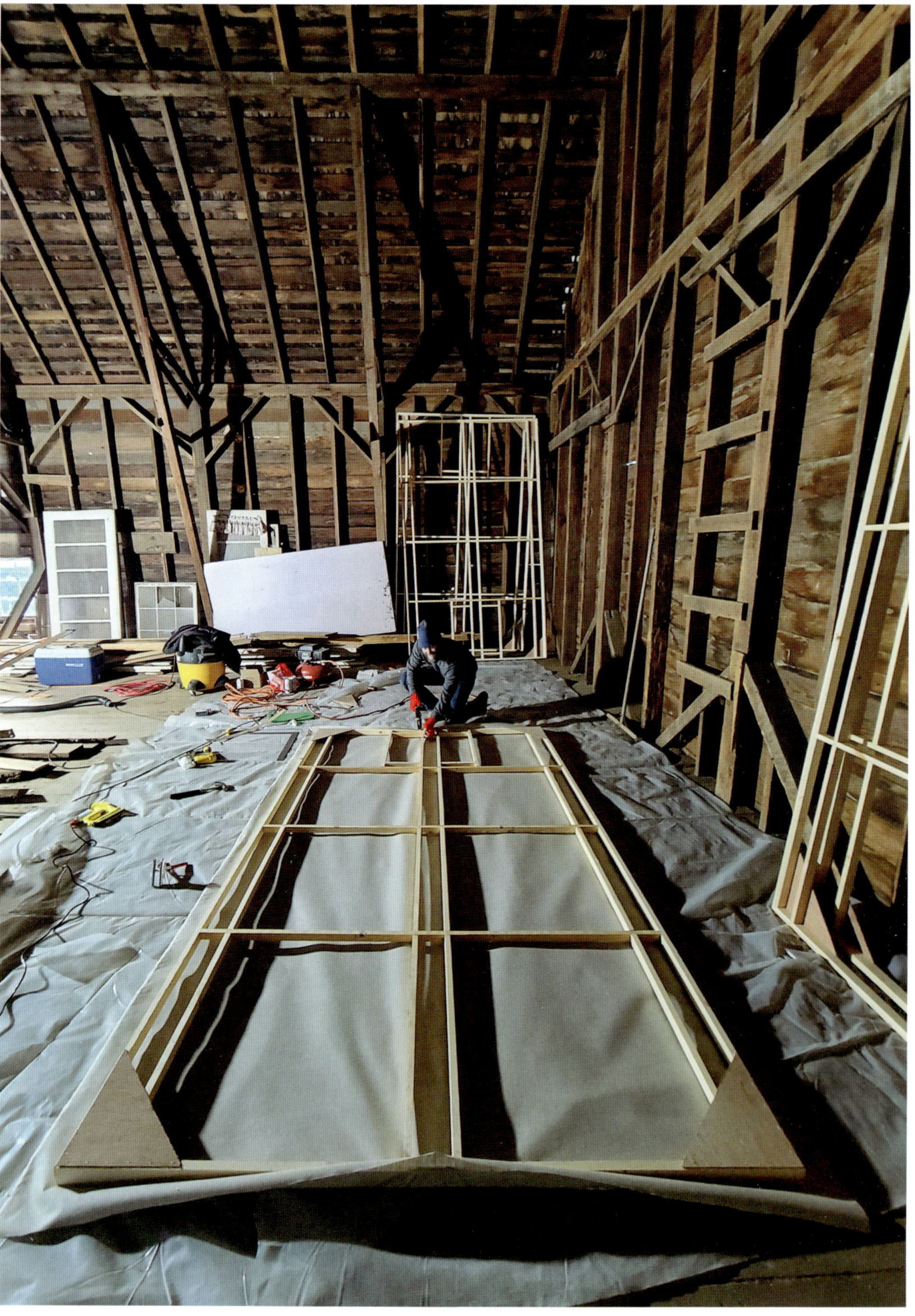

and that body, in abridged form and at a digital remove that, albeit not ideal, has become a very real component of—even a standard frame for—how contemporary artists must present themselves today. Instagram can be a kind of alembic through which all art is cut down to size, and what is left is a reduction that is, sometimes, truthful in its separations. Against the grain, it is entirely possible to distill some essentials from the infamous 1,080-by-1,080-pixel square—even if these essences are closer in spirit to Michelangelo Antonioni's film *Blow-Up* (1966) than to anything one might pick up in a conventional gallery space.

Fig. 11. Jack Bangerter helps Chowdhury stretch canvases for *Same Old Song*, December 5, 2021. Courtesy of the artist. Photo: Srijon Chowdhury

In 2020, I wrote of how the @boschbot account on Twitter could be doing more to further our appreciation of Hieronymus Bosch's *The Garden of Earthly Delights* (fig. 12) than most recent scholarship on it "by exposing and exploiting its extraordinary detail through a telescopic lens, in an approach that allows the observer to engage the work on a precritical, almost *prefrontal* level, while opening up new and previously unseen dimensions of an artwork that had become something of a floating signifier through overexposure."[1]

Chowdhury's Instagram affords many such intimations and close-ups. It goes from the amateurish to being strikingly intentional and well composed, and in so doing it presents the viewer with something rather like a lifestyle proposition. The painter's family is front and center, and the art is framed around them and the joys of their domestic life, rather than otherwise (fig. 13). There are four children, ranging in ages from toddlers to late teens; chickens, pigs, fluffy dogs—and friends—are manifested in a fairy-tale yard with no neighbors in view, dotted with painterly twilights and glistening, dew-spangled flowers. The center of this universe is Anna, his wife.

When I ask Chowdhury about her, he does not waver: "My wife is really, *really* beautiful," he says. "I kind of started painting portraits again because of how beautiful she is. It's so easy to want to paint her." They met through mutuals—enmeshment, again, as Chowdhurian motif—and it was love at first sight: "She walked into my house in the morning and I was like: 'Whoa.' And then she smiled, and she has a kind of sharp, vampire, scary tooth, and I was, 'OK: I'm in love.'" It would be perverse to think of such a brazen love of beauty as objectification: beauty is a heightened state, which Anna dependably provides to him as a subject of adoration—and study. And since beauty is its own virtue and thus affords a measure of invulnerability, Chowdhury has portrayed her in extremely vulnerable situations.

Among the most remarkable pieces in his entire catalogue is a portrait of her giving home water birth to their daughter Inez (2019; p. 64). The agony and ecstasy of labor are captured with explicitness and ambiguity in equal measure, in a painting that exploits the inherent tensions in Chowdhury's work by bringing them to surface. The pool water is a cosmogenetic swamp, with arms sinking like mangroves into primal ooze and bodies surging and emerging from it. Only Anna's head and torso are illuminated in an otherwise turbid tableau, her expression transfixed into the peak orgasm of a woman giving birth to new life, while being herself borne into motherhood. It is a rendering of childbirth as a total sex act.

Looking at his catalogue, I ask Chowdhury how he thinks about the differences between abstract and figurative painting. He says there are none, really: all painting is representative, or at least all of his is, even when it zooms in so much that the subject is distorted by propinquity. This, in turn, raises questions about portraiture as the art of representing others.

While he was in college, Chowdhury had a job as an artist at an amusement park, where he learned to think of people's faces in terms of relations between features. It took him a long time to unlearn the eye of the caricaturist. His attunement to relationships between parts is still there, but the desire for likeness has become less urgent: "Sometimes the best thing for a painting isn't that it looks true to life, or like the person you're depicting. Overworking something to make it look like the person can ruin the painting. It

Fig. 12. Hieronymus Bosch. *The Garden of Earthly Delights* triptych, 1490–1500. Grisaille, oil on oak panel. 73 1/10 × 128 1/5 in. Museo Nacional del Prado, Madrid, P002823. © Photographic Archive Museo Nacional del Prado

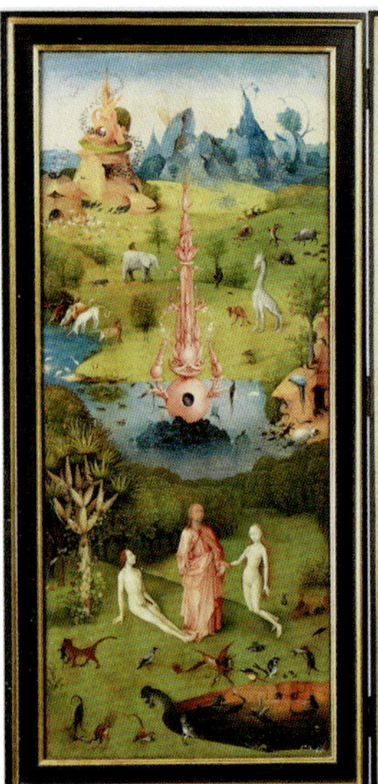
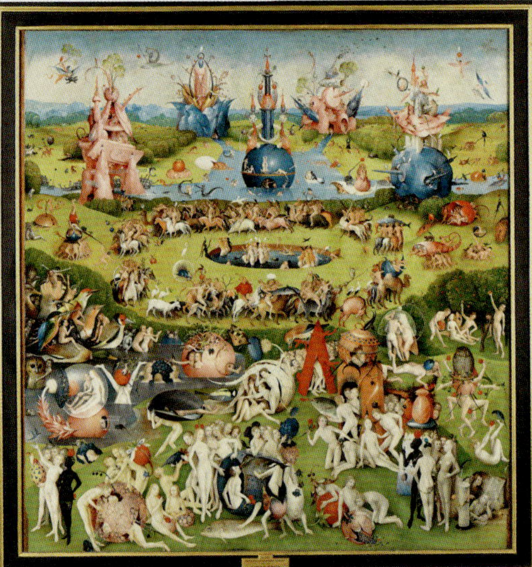
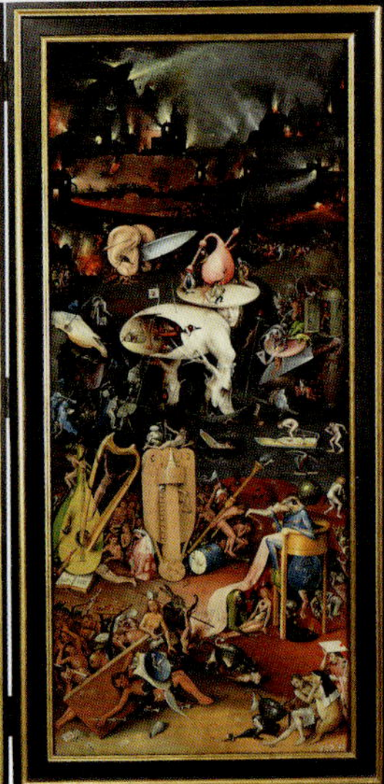

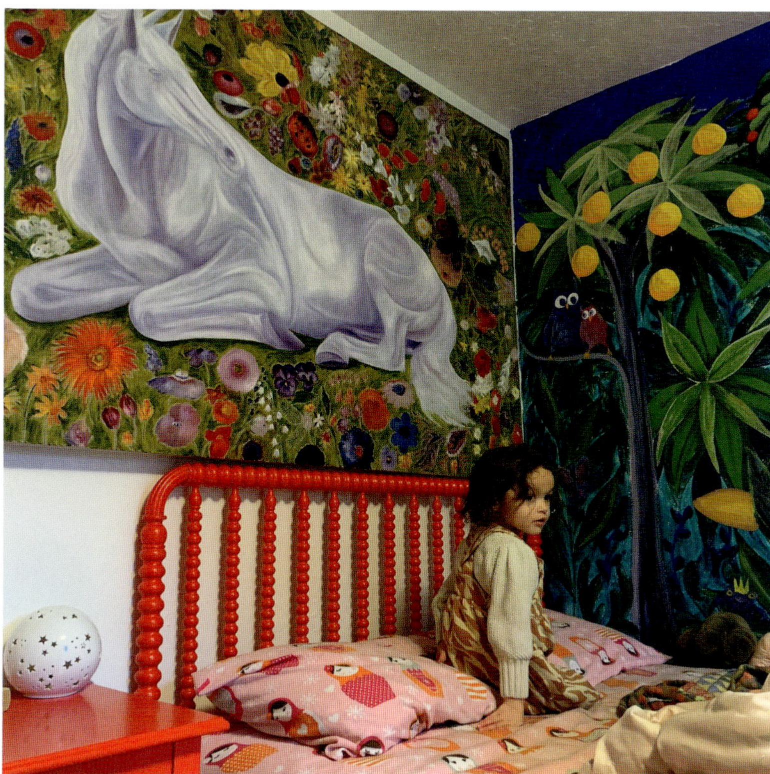

Fig. 13. Inez Chowdhury's bedroom, December 20, 2020. Courtesy of the artist. Photo: Anna Margaret

doesn't *matter* what the person looks like. As the portrait lives in time, likeness is increasingly irrelevant in the long run. All we have left, having shed our presences, are our representations."

This may not seem like an overtly political statement, but it casts an ancient relational shadow. Srijon Chowdhury is grazing the intimate distance of cave painting.

The Miracle of Death: On the Work of Srijon Chowdhury

SJ Cowan

A Rococo spirit possesses the work of Srijon Chowdhury. It pulls in two directions. His work not only leads us into this Late Baroque movement (ca. 1680–1750), but it advances us beyond it as well. That is, Chowdhury's work provides a way of rereading the innocence, extravagance, and playfulness of the Rococo as a reflection of something much more grim; and, at the same time, allows us to conceive of the crises of our own time as expressions of something miraculous, as something divine made manifest in our earthy presence. This spirit can already be sensed in his earlier work. It is as if he has prepared a new way, for instance, for Thomas Gainsborough's *The Blue Boy* (fig. 1) and François Boucher's *Diane sortant du bain* (Bath of Diana) (fig. 2) to catch up to us. When comparing their compositional structure, for example, to his own *Boy* (2018; p. 49) and *Birth* (2019; p. 64), the similarities are apparent. A young boy, standing in a shimmering blue suit against a background awash in green and murky red. A nude woman, in recline; the face of another directed toward her genitals that have been obscured from our view. But this is only the surface.

Fig. 1. Thomas Gainsborough. *The Blue Boy*, ca. 1770. Oil on canvas. 70⅝ × 48¾ × 1 in. Huntington Library, Art Museum, and Botanical Gardens, 21.1 © Huntington Art Collections /© Huntington Library, Art Museum, and Botanical Gardens, San Marino, CA/Bridgeman Images

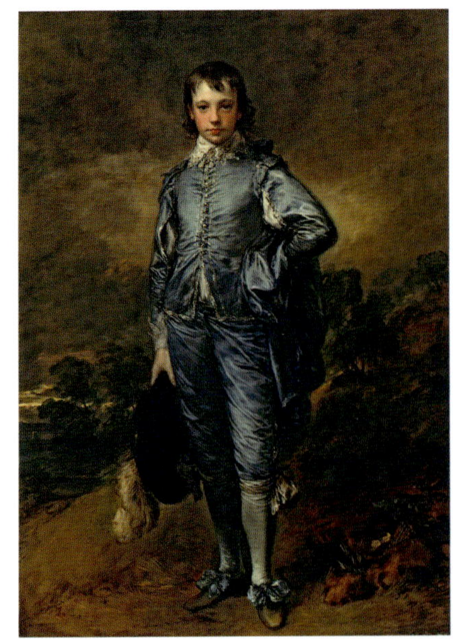

More substantially, Chowdhury has rendered, on the one hand, the living prominence still occupied by these *figurae* today, and on the other, the means for their vital impulse to become perverse enough to match our present. The blue boy, once self-possessed, dashing, and ripe, now stands nauseated, doing his best to keep his footing, glowering and tensed, compulsorily staring into the eye of the viewer. And unlike Diana, our subject in *Birth*—clearly no longer a virgin—cannot get out of her bath, is stuck, forever apart from the idyllic, in a moment of indeterminate, erotic grief: ecstasy or agony? In fact, Chowdhury's *Birth* even provides a helpful key to reading the peripheral violence active in Boucher's version. For Boucher, Diana offers a trace of the truly human, an ideal type, in the way she transcends the earth. It is true that Diana sits centrally within a forest scene. Yet she also sits removed from it, almost glowing, protected from the crudeness of nature surrounding her: strewn carcasses of small animals; a dog's anus and swollen testicles protruding into view.

By contrast, for Chowdhury, what Diana was meant to represent has become the moment of birth—something shadowy, almost like a dream, an expression of the animal relief that is immanent to our capacity to transcend ourselves. To transcend not by stripping away the crudeness of our lives, but by engaging such crudeness at once reflectively, and yet no less forcibly than a dog or dead rabbit. Chowdhury preserves (and shines a new light upon) the surplus of drama that gives Boucher's and Gainsborough's works their still-recognizable sense of originality. If the Late Baroque gives us a positive image of the burgeoning excess that would come to define what it means to live and think like a modern, then Chowdhury provides for us the negative imprint of that selfsame excess, pressing against and contesting its limits.

To name the Rococo is to stir up a variety of perplexing questions about the conceptual bases, the motivations, and the modes of production involved in this immense and elusive cultural movement. Very often, it has been understood as a moment of decline,

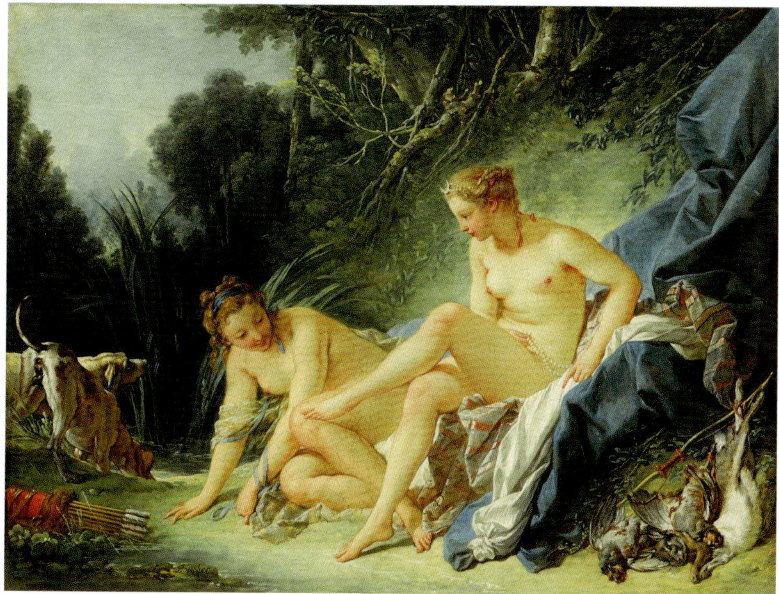

Fig. 2. François Boucher. *Diane sortant du bain* (Bath of Diana), 1742. Oil on canvas, 22 × 28 7/10 in. Musée du Louvre, Paris, INV2712. Photo: Mathieu Rabeau © RMN-Grand Palais / Art Resource, NY

the degenerate finality of the Baroque era. In this view, the Rococo stands as an outpouring of extravagance by the frivolous elite classes at the dawn of the Enlightenment. Perhaps. That may be sufficient to explain much of what is Late Baroque. But, in reading the Rococo as a moment of closure—as an ending—we bar ourselves from thinking of it as a possible new beginning, a mode of true innovation in thought. In *Same Old Song*, Chowdhury's exhibition at the Frye Art Museum, the Rococo spirit appears in this alternative mode: less as a moment that rests in our past and more as a messenger of our possible future, one wherein the crises of the world can be viewed as the miracle of existence made manifest, the miracle of existence working itself out.

Crises and miracle.

The crises are easy to spot. Upon entering his exhibition, one enters further into the sense of gloom that hovers over the everyday. From corner to corner, the sense of dread, death, fire, etc., etc., etc., is engrossing, profound: if we're not looking at climate change, then it's the implosion of capitalism; if it's not the rise of fascism, then it's the coldness of the administrative, logistical, and scientized logics that now characterize our normal patterns of being; and so on. It is a sorry state when such a list has, as it has today, become clichéd, either because (as believers in these crises would have it) all these things are waiting to come crashing down upon us, or because (as deniers would have it) we have deluded ourselves into a form of mass psychosis or have fallen into a groveling servitude before the state, from which we cannot escape.

Adorno taught us that every work of art is, in itself, the nexus of a problem.[1] And this is certainly true for *Same Old Song*. This problem was not simply *how to interpret a work*, even if every artwork poses its own unique interpretive challenges. More significantly, the problem a work of art represents is born out of the tensions and inconsistencies of the conditions of the present. But the artwork does not stop at reflecting the world back to us; the world it shows us is as much like the world as it is unlike the world. That is, in the very act of reflection, the work of art distorts the scene, giving us an image of our world in which nothing is changed, yet everything is different. Chowdhury shares a surprising, stubborn, and difficult problem with his viewers: "What good is making art if the world is going to hell?" Through this question, he offers us a chance to recognize the grim structure of our world as a true revelation and uncovering, an *apokálypsis*, of the miracle we inhabit. Yes, the crises are easy to spot in Chowdhury's work. But what is the miracle made manifest in them? And where is it to be found? These are the questions I want to approach in the following pages. To begin, we must briefly consider the type of world Chowdhury portrays for us.

Leibniz was among the great thinkers who carried us into the Late Baroque.[2] If the Rococo spirit possessing Chowdhury's work takes us, at once, into and beyond the Late Baroque, then it should come as no surprise to find that Leibnizian concepts provide the means for a fruitful engagement with Chowdhury's work. Consider, for instance, Leibniz's notion that we live in "the best of all possible worlds." Given what Leibniz thought he could rationally deduce about the nature of God, he concluded that there is no other real possibility for the world, except that it be the best possible one. Since God is, he explains, all knowing, all powerful, and all benevolent, it cannot be that God could (or would) create the world otherwise. Importantly, God knows the world ought not to be created as the most beautiful or the most ideal. Chowdhury knows this, too.

There is always a temptation to fashion things too beautifully. Such temptation must give us pause. And in the moment of that pause, comes hesitation. The hesitation says, *Do not begin with so much beauty*. For if we do, it will not last long: we put ourselves at risk of undoing whatever it is we create, even before it has come to fruition. We may seek for something that exceeds the conditions of our lives, our limitations, our finitude; but all we can ever find are more *things*, limited and finite. The irony of ideal types!—Their failure to persist. The moment they take their first breath, they crumble, having no place within our air.

Same Old Song can be appreciated as a sustained meditation on the disappointment that sits in the heart of our ideals. An almost palpable uneasiness tempers the mood of Chowdhury's paintings, a sense as large and foreboding as the enclosure they create within the gallery. The deep reds entice us inward, and the subtle layering of imagery and paint draws us even further into what begins to feel like a three-dimensional space sitting atop the flat surface of his canvas. In these works, the ideal types of painting's history—nude women, still lifes of flowers, birth, and light—are rendered hollow. Their features are not given the glory they typically demand. Rather, they are shown arrested in a standstill: indifferent to the moments of contact they make with other figures in the scene, indifferent to the fact that their warmth is not warm enough to thaw their frozen apathy, indifferent to their very own indifference that they so readily put on show for the viewer.

Chowdhury understands that the inability for our ideals to be made real is a testament not to their purity (as if earth and flesh corroded them), but rather to their sickness. And so it was not beauty, Leibniz explains, that God chose to maximize when creating the world. Instead, we learn that God chose a world that is simplest in hypotheses (or laws) and richest in phenomena. In doing so, God resists the possibility of *this* or *that* ideal and instead calculates a balance to allow for as many things to be put together as can be. These formulations by Leibniz have made him famous for his optimism. However, there is nothing about this reasoning alone that renders it optimistic. Yes, if there were not a best among all possible worlds, then God would not have created a world at all. But saying something is the "best" is one thing, and deeming it to be "good" is another.

The important twist on Leibnizian thought that Chowdhury's work attunes us to is the pessimistic tone in which the very same thought can be pronounced. *This* is the best of all possible worlds? *This world?* Our world is the world wherein ideals never come to fruition. For Chowdhury, the interplay of our ideals and the necessary dissatisfaction they breed is key to understanding the strange, human phenomenon of always striving for something better—something like progress, something like happiness, something like peace—but producing something worse, like decline, destruction, anxiety, and uncertainty. Yet we must not, Chowdhury's work teaches us, seek to overcome the worse in favor of the better. In fact, held within his work is the insight that hating our destructiveness is part and parcel to hating life itself. Only in death are we given a life freed unto the miracle that it is.

For Leibniz, the question of the nature of the miraculous logically follows his argument about the bestness of our world. Likewise, the notion of the miracle can connect with the strain of pessimistic thought expressed in Chowdhury's *Same Old Song*. For Leibniz, the world is completely balanced and made orderly by God. In order to avoid falling into the trap of suggesting that miracles somehow occur behind the back of the conditions necessarily holding our world together, Leibniz argued that miracles occur with respect to the universal, natural order established by God. In other words, miracles do not exceed natural laws (as is very often thought)—they conform to them. What is particularly interesting about Leibniz's insistence on the naturalization of the miraculous is the way it allows us to view miracles as something as near to us as anything else in the realm of nature. There is an almost Romantic ring to this thought. And while Leibniz was not guided by a Romantic impulse, Chowdhury certainly is.

The romance of *Same Old Song* is found in its dealings with death. In fact, a prevailing theme in this work is the attempt to come to grips with an intimacy with death. It is often said that no one experiences their own death, since it marks the end of experience in general. However, Chowdhury's world of images reminds us that this is not true at all. Though we share much of ourselves with others, when it comes to death, we are (in Leibniz's terms) monads: beings existing at an infinite remove from one another, windowless rooms from which nothing can leave and into which nothing can enter. We all experience death every day, even our own. With death, we are buried within ourselves: our external signals, gestures, and voices are nothing but indefinite and useless channels for crossing the gap that separates us from one another. For all that can be experienced with others, perhaps what is utterly incommunicable in life is the simplest hour of them all—the one of muteness, the one of death—of one's own death. It is what guides us into our futures, and what prods us into our own interior worlds. This is why, for instance, "a deceased person," in Novalis's words, "is a person that has been raised to the absolutely mysterious state."[3] Chowdhury presses into this Romantic idea, illustrating for us that death is the miracle and pure mystery of existence.

Death is a miracle. Our *miracle*.

Consider, for example, the two large paintings of eyes in *Same Old Song* (2022; pp. 80–81). Both eyes contain symbols of hopes, dreams, and open potentiality: in one, there is an infant in a scene of birth; in the other, a morning glory. The eyes are split chasms, simultaneously ocular and vaginal. The canal through which the infant and the flower emerge both delivers them into and provides them a vision of the hellscape in which they find themselves. As with most of Chowdhury's figures, their futurity is called into question: already the innocence of the infant's face is marked by an air of indifference; the new growth of the morning glory is a sprout of hope, already being cut down. The workings of death that surround them in the exhibition already constitute the fate of flower and infant. The cruelty of existence lies in the fact that what is most miraculous brings the real sorrow of the end, but not the end itself.

The interiority that the miracle of death brings upon us, all our lives, is a consciousness of anticipation of an end, of real sorrow, even when no dying in the true sense has taken place. In this exhibition, Chowdhury ultimately presents viewers with a gathering-together of imagery from—an interiorization of—his earlier work. Again, there are birth, fire, demon-like figures, melting and struggling bodies; blank, almost hypnotized stares; flowers and foliage, an overdose of red—an amalgamation of all that one might expect to come from Chowdhury's hand. Yet the work in this exhibition does not function as a survey and development of these subjects, as if Chowdhury were conducting an expansive variation on his previous themes. Instead, the work works to summarize and transform the stages of his own history. Picking up self-references and self-quotations, and rearranging them, Chowdhury's struggle is to perform a retrospective exhibition for himself, one in which his previous work folds in upon itself, attempting to internalize itself, but at the same time threatening to collapse. The process of interiorization is one that, quite literally, can be found in the way his paintings are composed and arranged. Eyes, a mouth, ears, a nose. The entire room is now host to a face.

The perspective is disorienting. As viewers, are we meant to be situated inside the skull, looking out of the orifices? Or are we outside the skin, with the face being warped to surround us completely? In either case, the process of interiorization cannot be escaped. If the former, then viewers have no choice but to sit internal to the work, surrounded by a nightmare of figures pressing themselves into the inside of which—because it is only thanks to them that there is an inside to speak of at all—they already belong. And if it is the latter, then we have become enfolded into the head, occupying a typically external space that has inverted itself, and so become an interior. As within a monad, we find ourselves within a living mirror of our universe.

Chowdhury's method for producing *Same Old Song* gives clear priority to patience. His attention to detail; the amount of imagery (both subtle and spectacular) that he fits within each frame; and the density of information that he conveys all bear witness to this fact. Importantly, the line of questioning that his work makes possible, i.e., that while this may be the best of all possible worlds, it is still not a "good" one, presents itself in the form of an ambiguity, exposing at once the polarities: curiosity and unease, hope and dread, etc. What is more, for Chowdhury, the points of ambiguity do not represent moments of contrast. That is, his is not a battle of hope *or* dread, curiosity *or* unease. Rather, the phenomenon he captures is the overriding power of all that is indistinguishable: hope is found in the image of dread, and dread, within the hope. Throughout the exhibition, we are caught within an overflow into an interior, in which the present is pregnant with the future, and the future is pregnant with death, the miracle of existence.

Chowdhury's work affords us an opportunity for thought. In *Same Old Song*, the crises of our world are not presented as sources of fear. Instead, the Rococo spirit possessing his work calls upon us to celebrate the perverse exorbitance of all that is miraculous about our world. While our excessiveness may not be as innocent, playful, and careless as was depicted in the Late Baroque, we can, nonetheless, embrace our crises as our own miracle. Denying our crises is a way of refusing the miracle of existence, of resisting the mystery of the divine. For death, in being our miracle, is our guiding light beyond ourselves, into our future, and within ourselves, into our own being. Dead figures, hands offering gestures of significance, utopic visions of life now burning, and the rare glimmers of light shrouded in the darkness they presuppose: Does not a room full of darkness already represent the possibility of the room, now well lit?

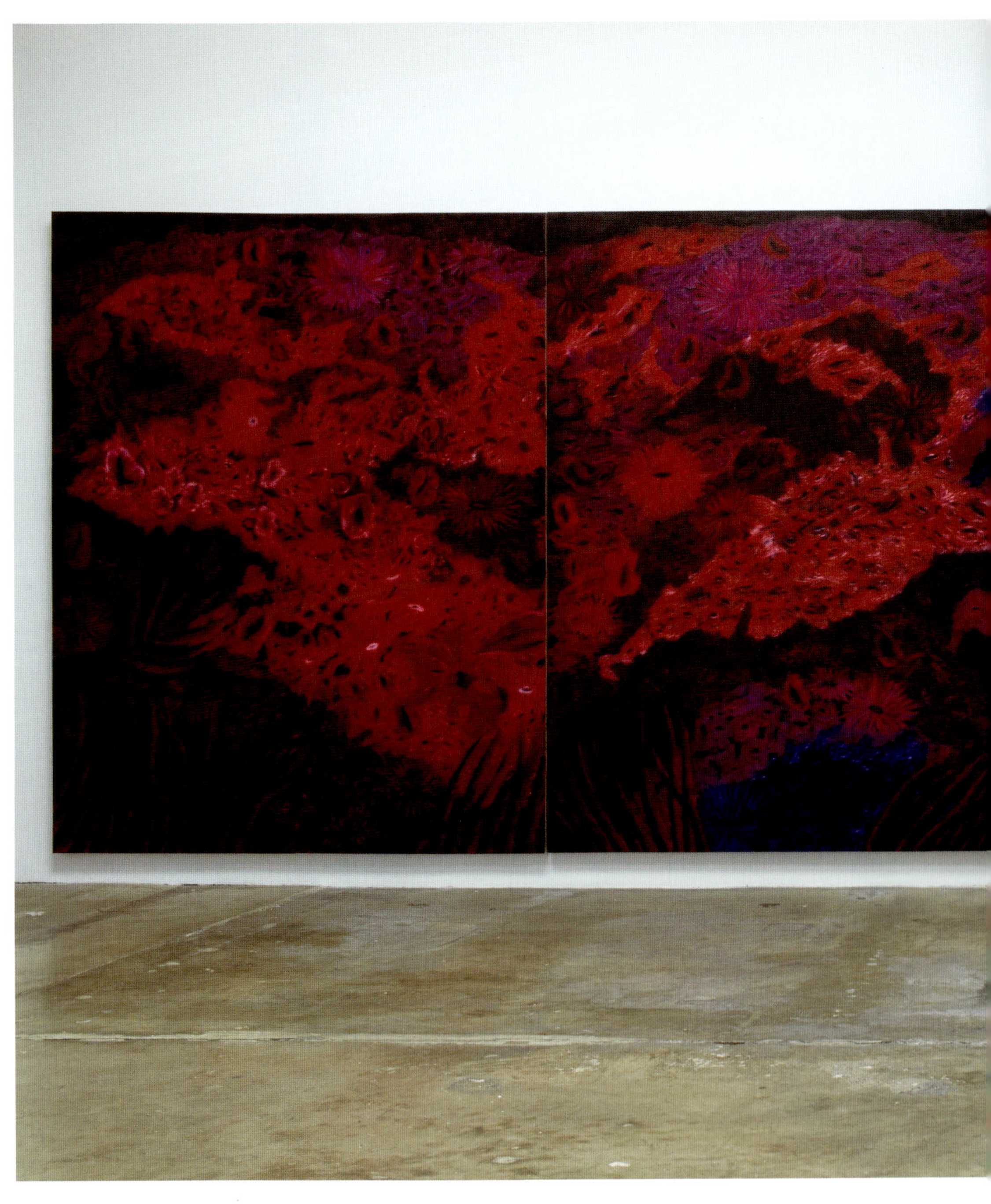

The Garden, 2014. Oil on linen. 96 × 72 in. Installation view from *Srijon Chowdhury: The Garden*, Klowden Mann, Los Angeles. Courtesy of the artist. Photo: Lee Thompson

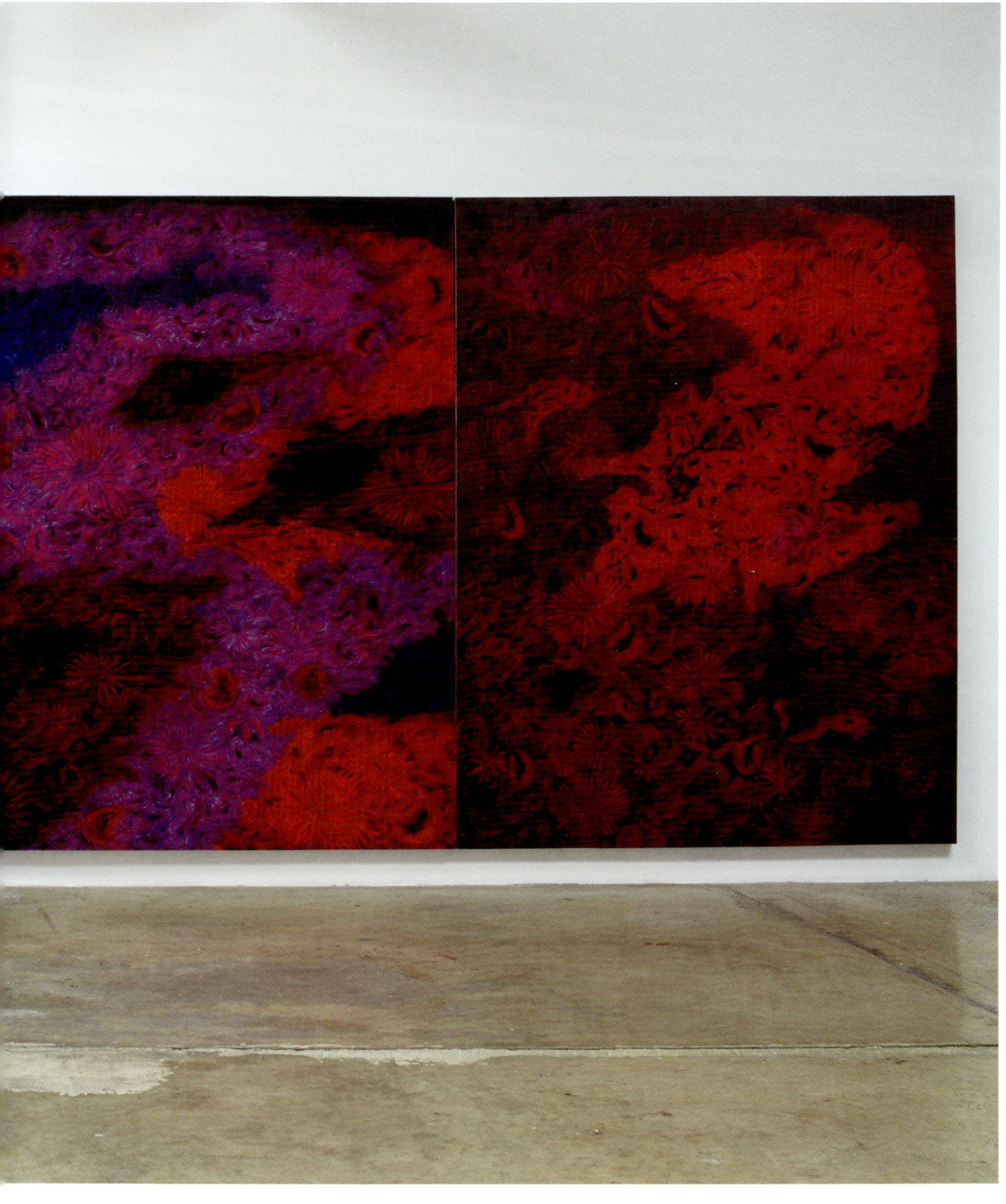

Making a painting, 2016. Oil on linen. 60¼ × 48¼ in. Courtesy of Ciaccia Levi, Paris-Milan.
Photo: Lee Thompson

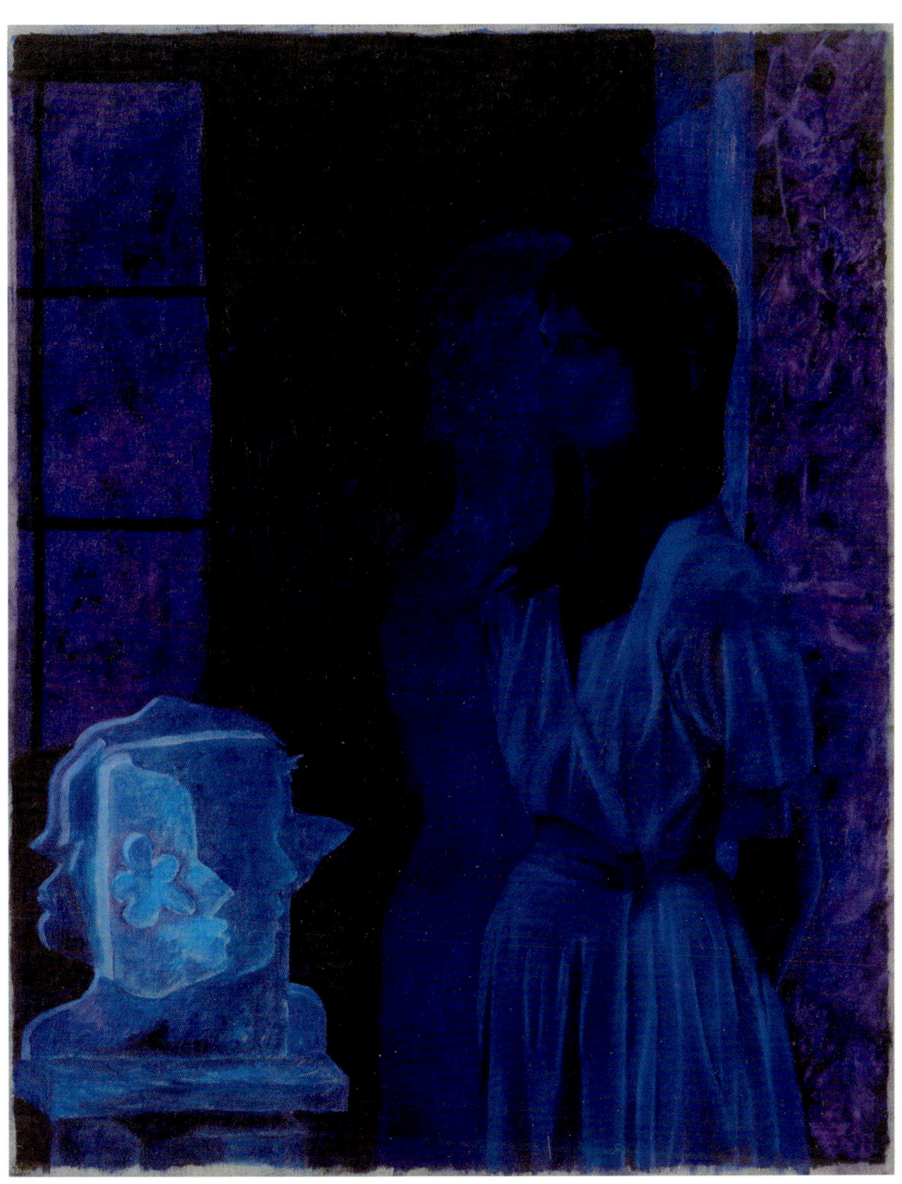

Katy with "Portraits" at her opening at Cherry and Martin, 2016. Oil on linen. 41 × 31 in.
Private collection. Photo: Lee Thompson

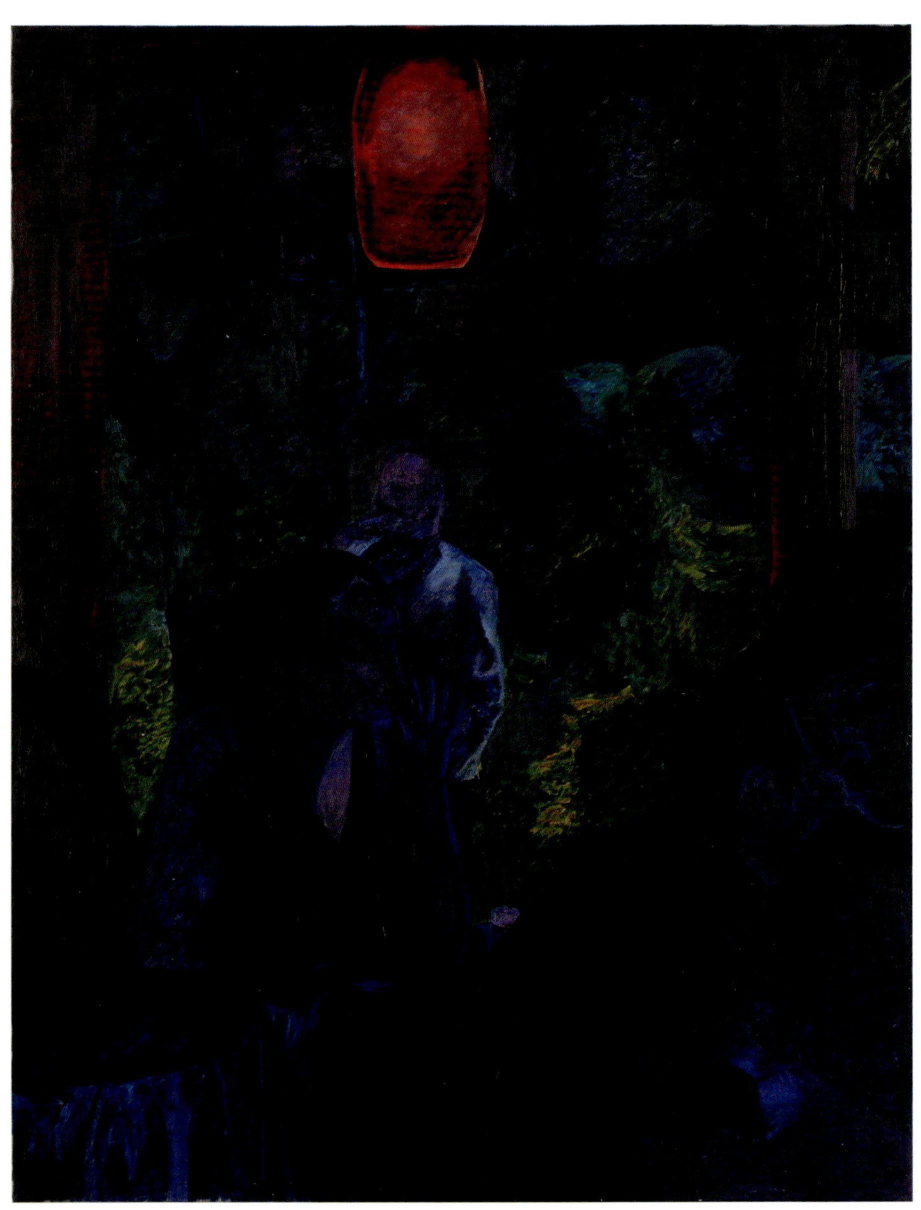

Jack smoking outside Masa, 2016. Oil on linen. 41 × 31 in. Collection of the artist.
Photo: Lee Thompson

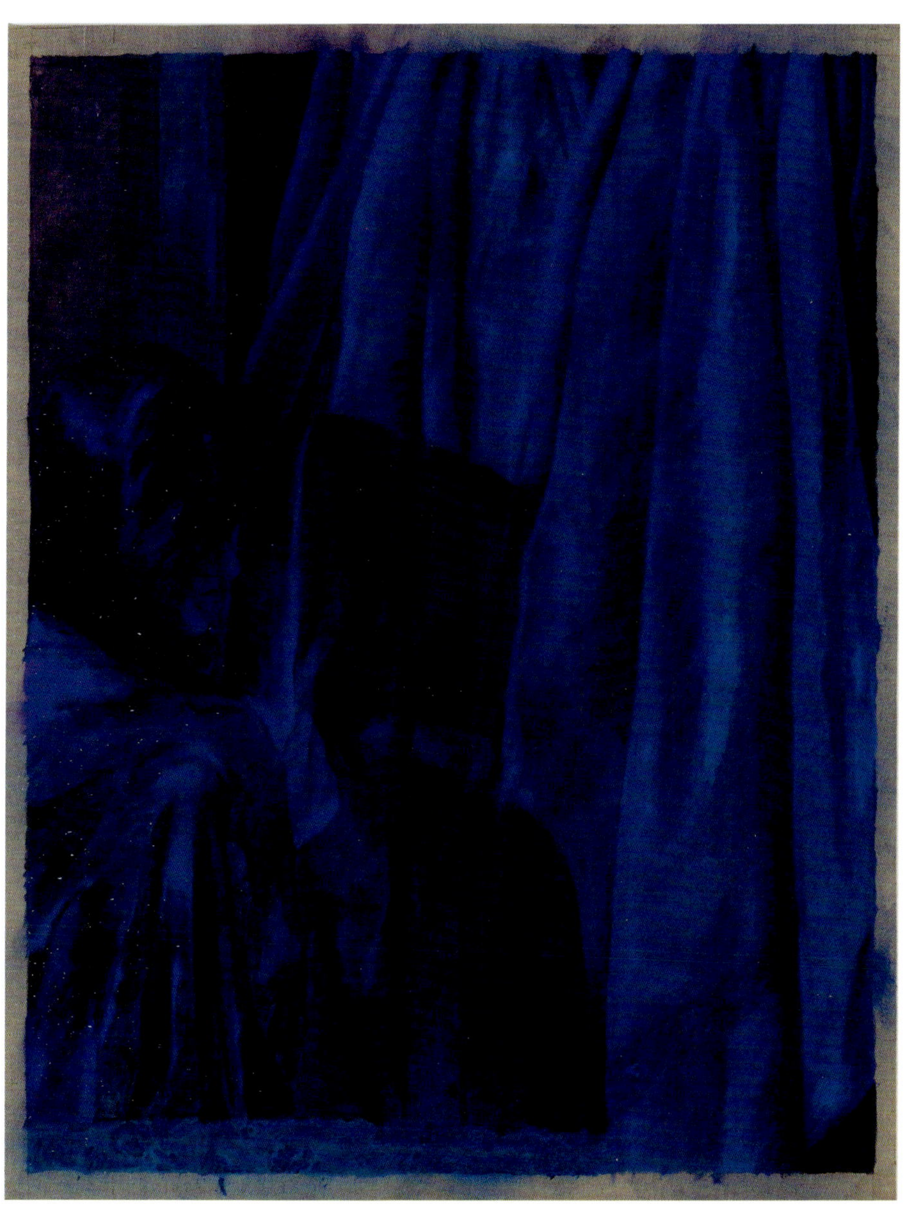

Anna drying her hair on the towels hanging from our bedroom door, 2016. Oil on linen. 42 × 32 in.
Private collection. Photo: Lee Thompson

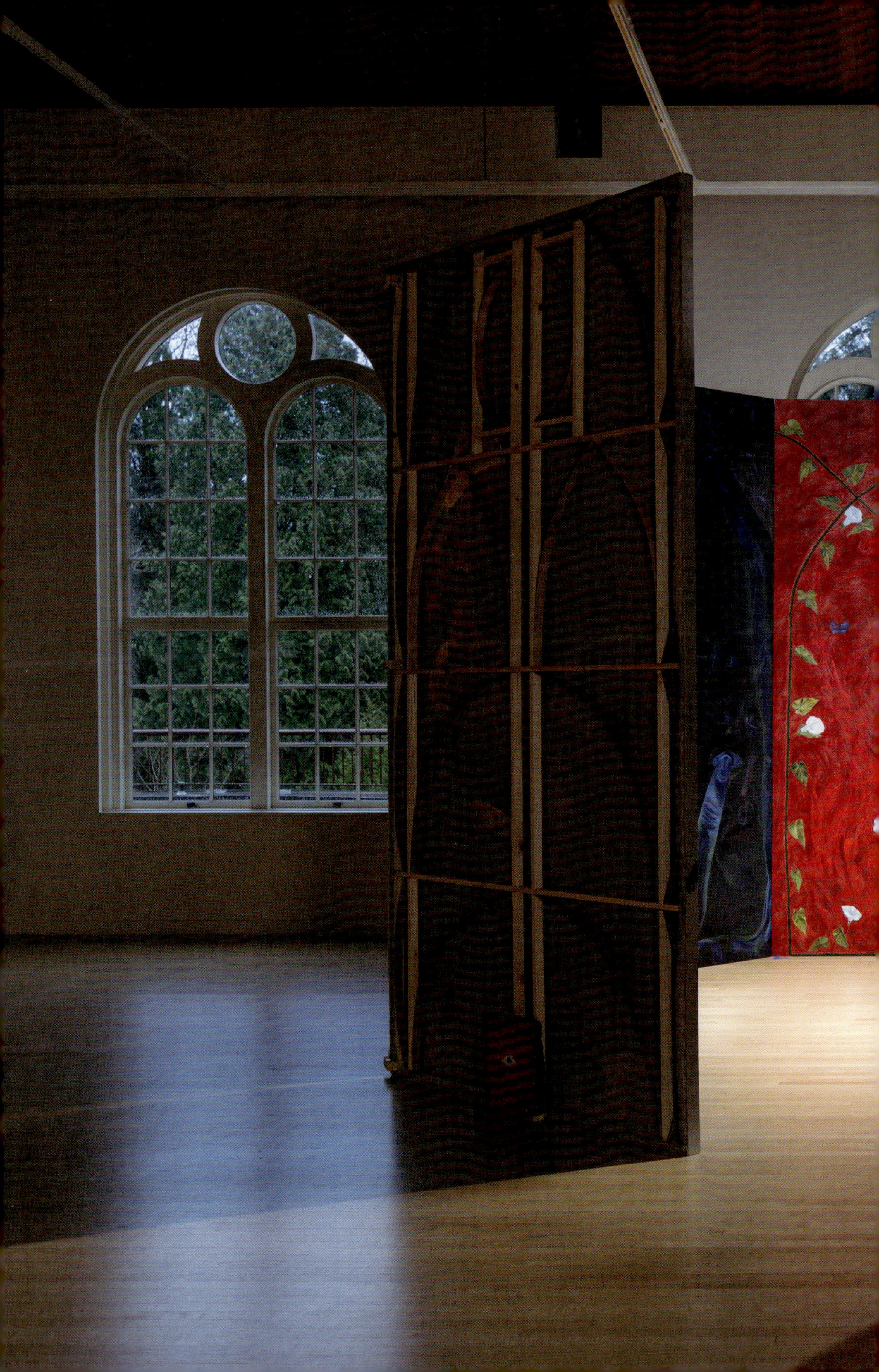

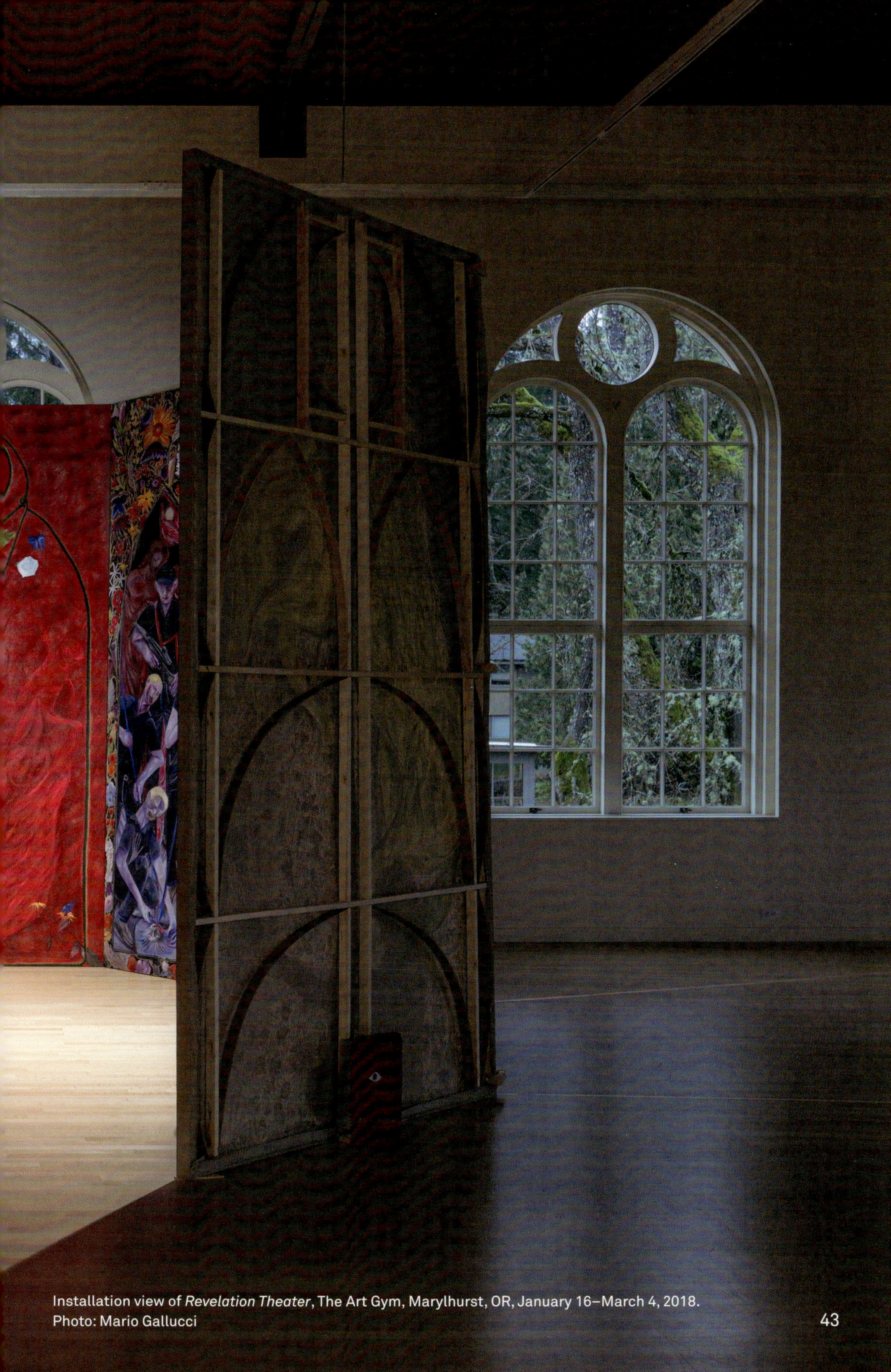

Installation view of *Revelation Theater*, The Art Gym, Marylhurst, OR, January 16–March 4, 2018.
Photo: Mario Gallucci

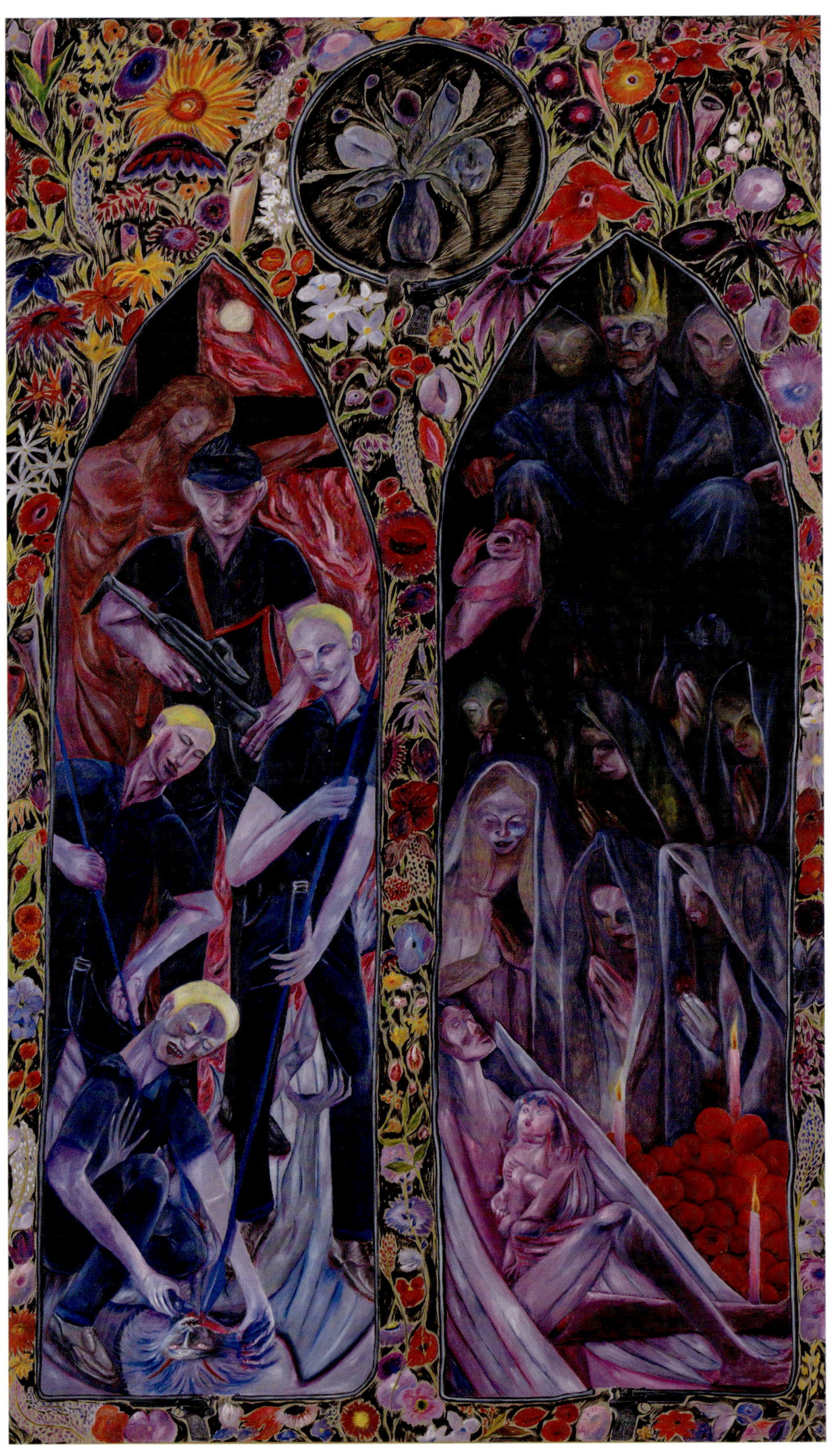

Revelation Theater (Fool), 2017. Oil on linen. 126 × 72 in. Courtesy of Ciaccia Levi, Paris-Milan. Photo: Mario Gallucci

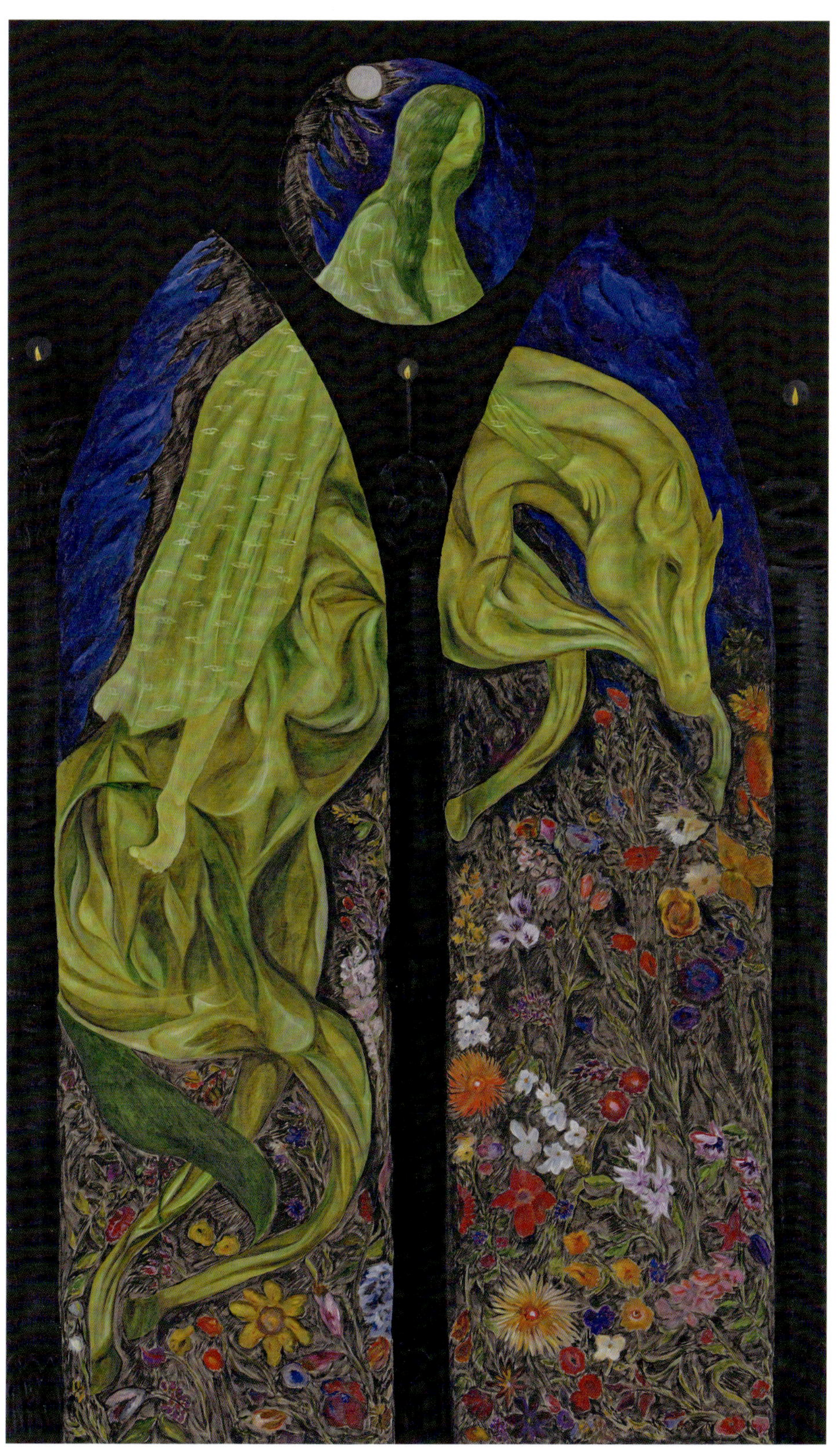

Revelation Theater (Horsemen), 2017. Oil on linen. 126 × 72 in. Courtesy of Ciaccia Levi, Paris-Milan.
Photo: Mario Gallucci

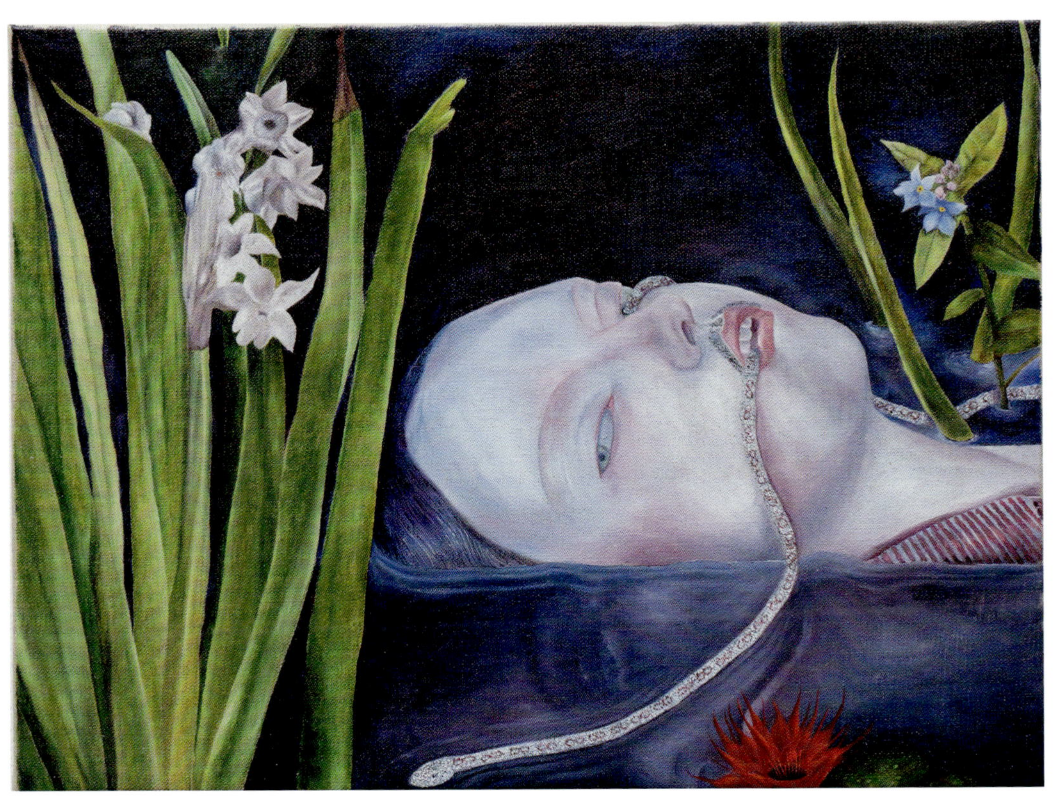

 Ophelia, 2018. Oil on linen. 12 × 16 in. Private collection. Photo: Mario Gallucci

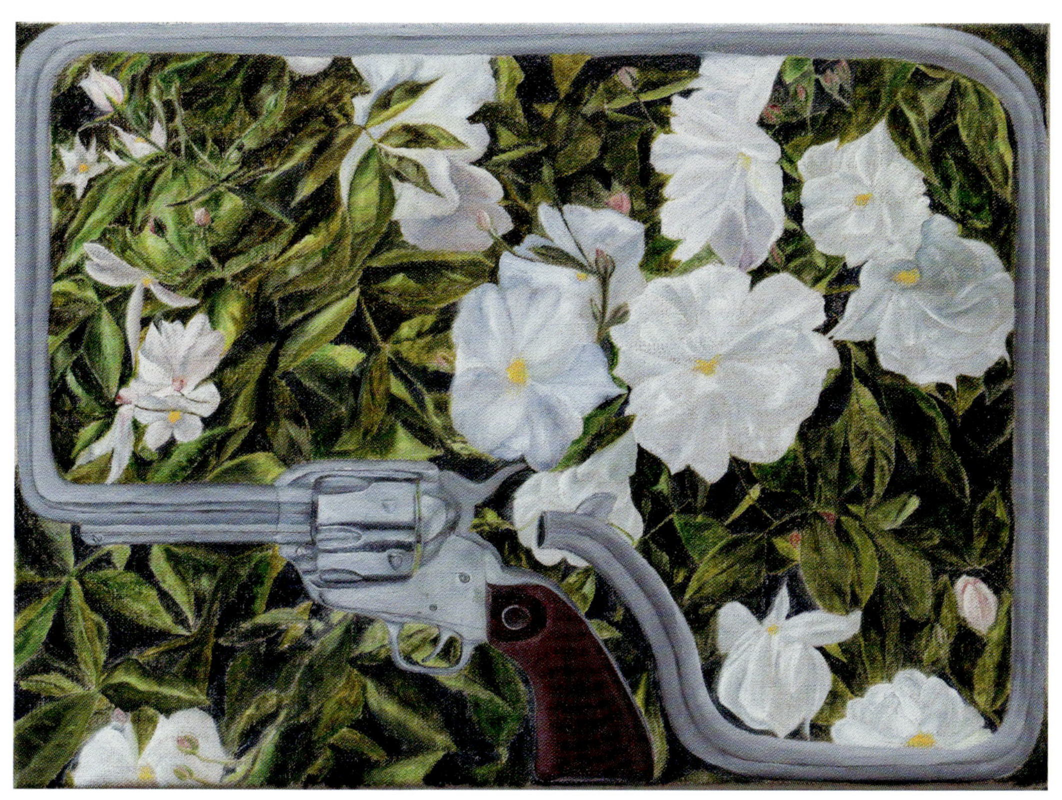

White Roses, 2018. Oil on linen. 12 × 16 in. Private collection. Photo: Mario Gallucci

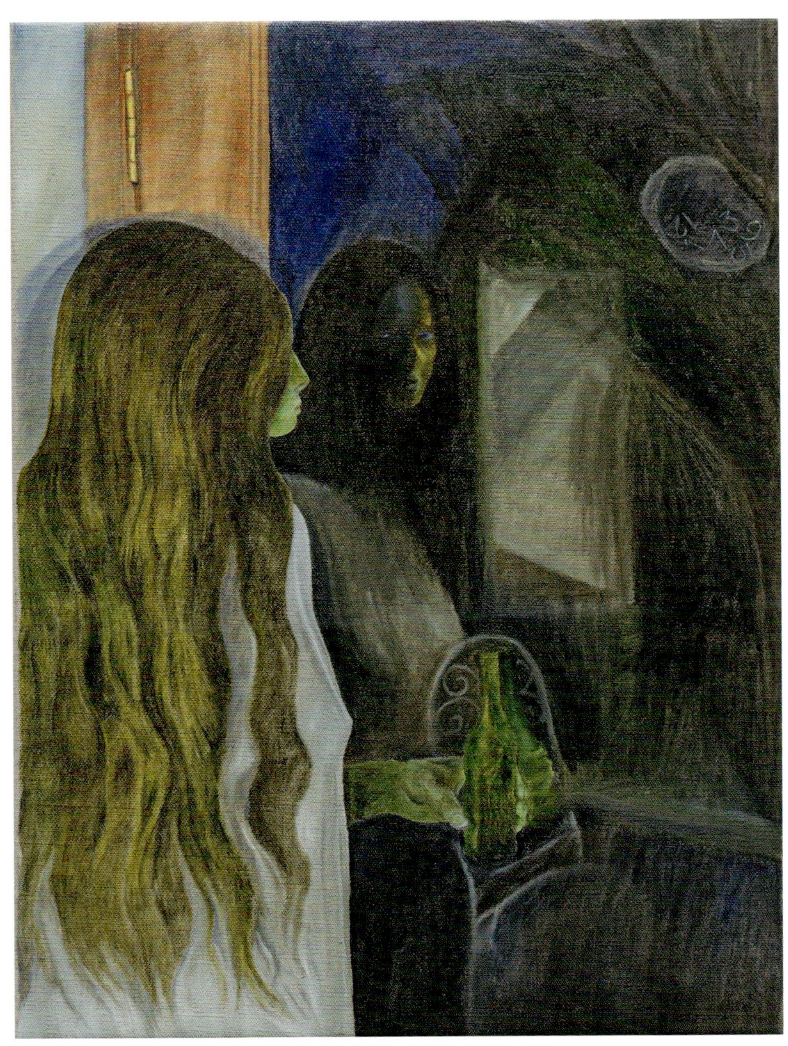

 Mirror, 2018. Oil on linen. 16 × 12 in. Private collection. Photo: Mario Gallucci

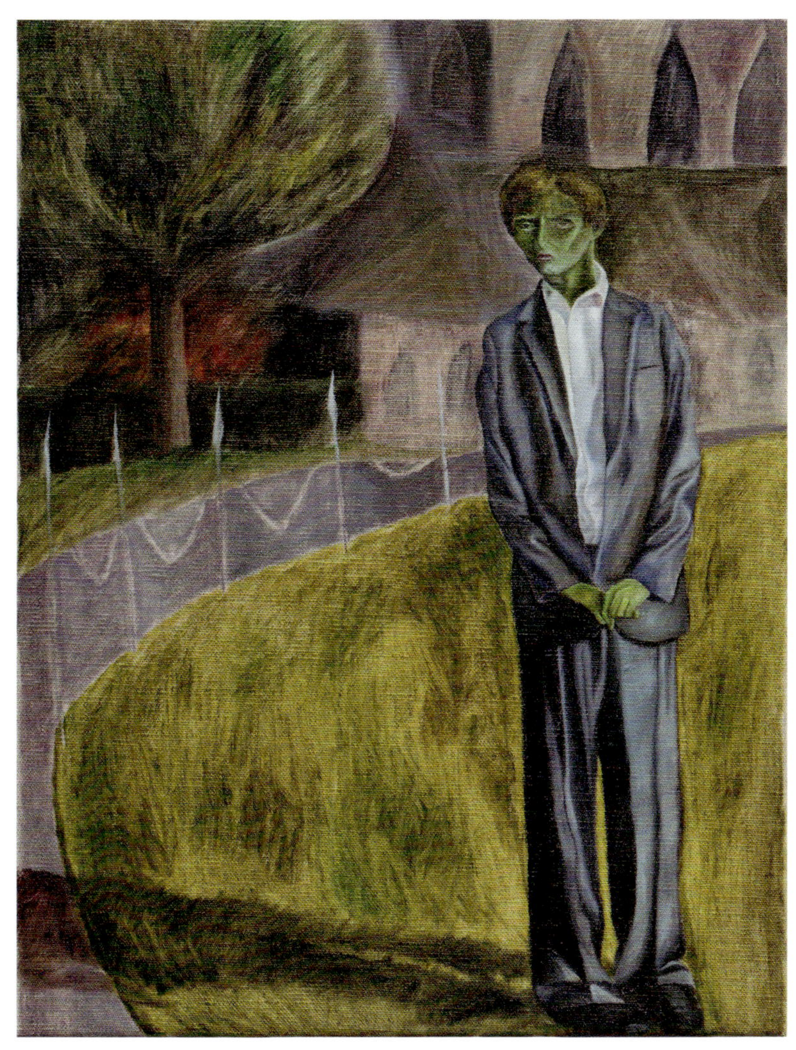

Boy, 2018. Oil on linen. 16 × 12 in. Private collection. Photo: Mario Gallucci

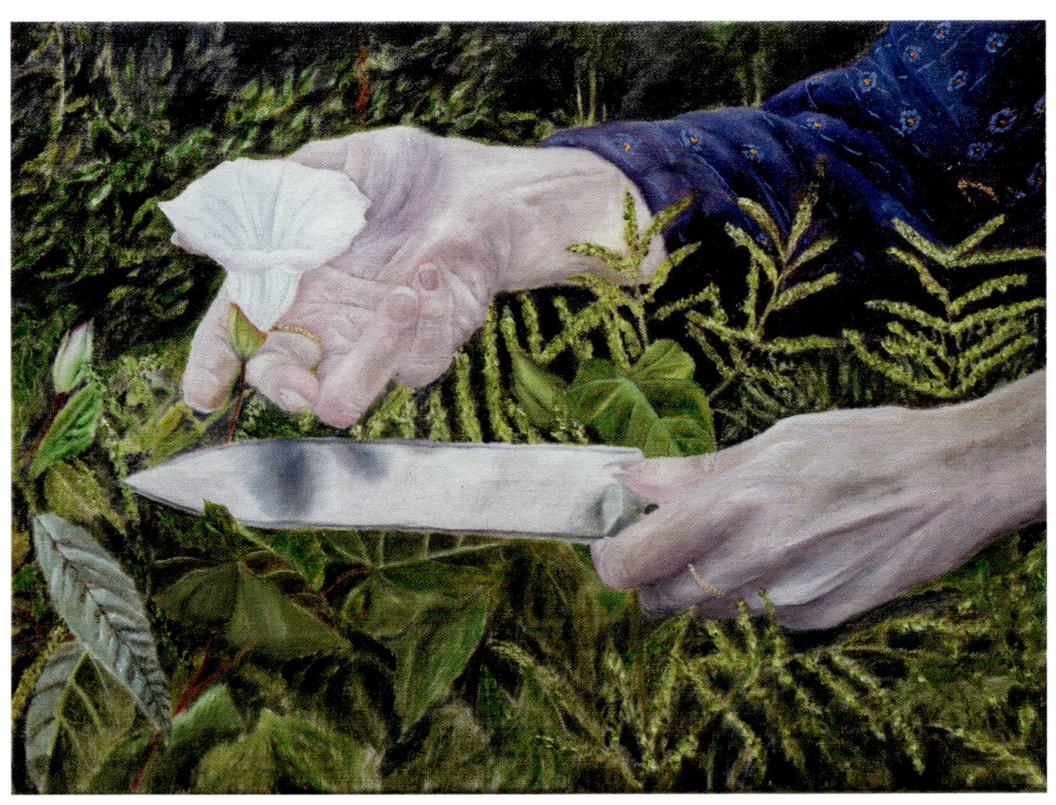

 Morning Glory, 2018. Oil on linen. 12 × 16 in. Private collection. Photo: Mario Gallucci

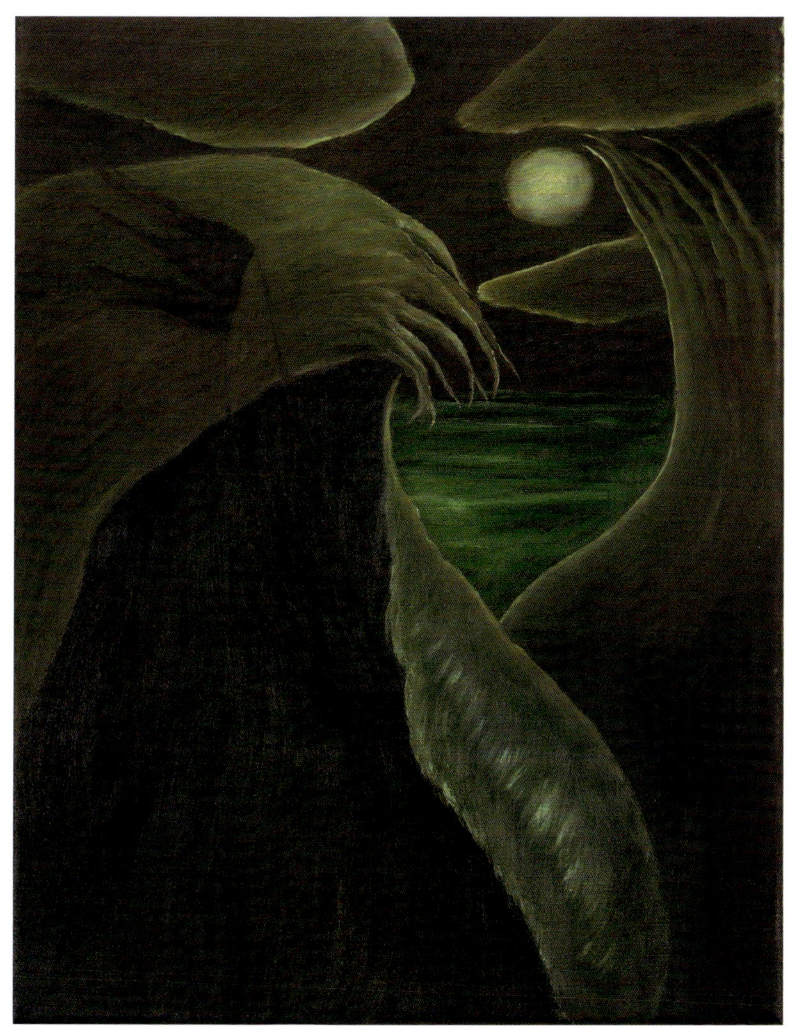

Hurricane, 2018. Oil on linen. 16 × 12 in. Private collection. Photo: Aurélien Mole

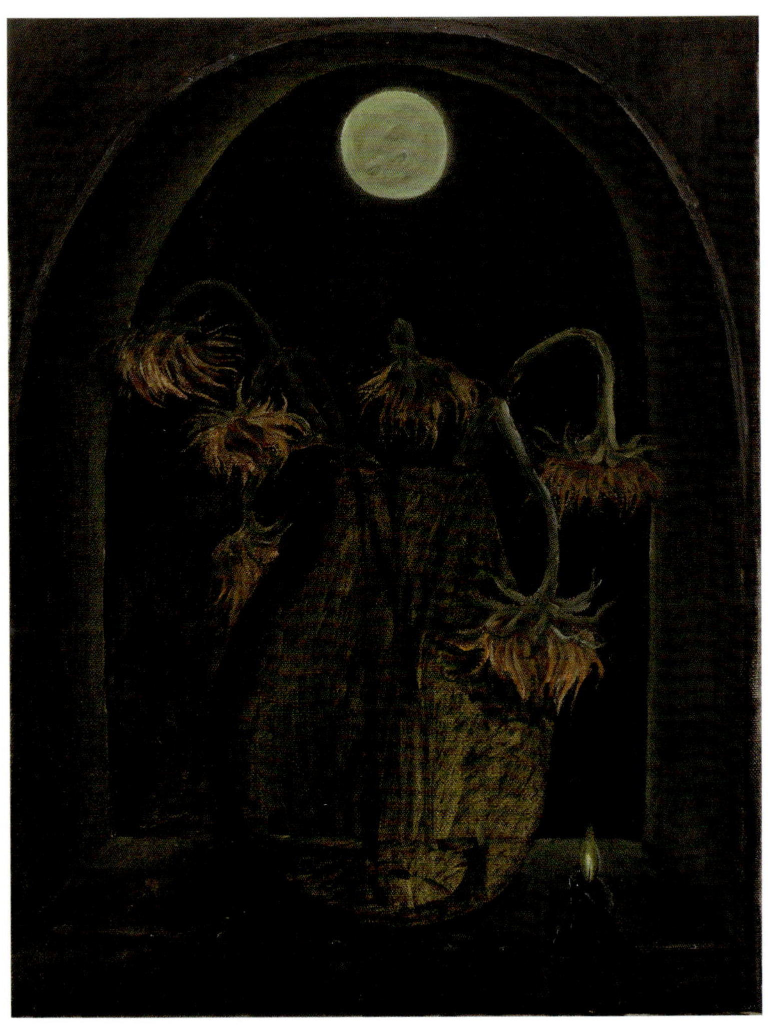

 Green Vase, 2018. Oil on linen. 16 × 12 in. Private collection. Photo: Aurélien Mole

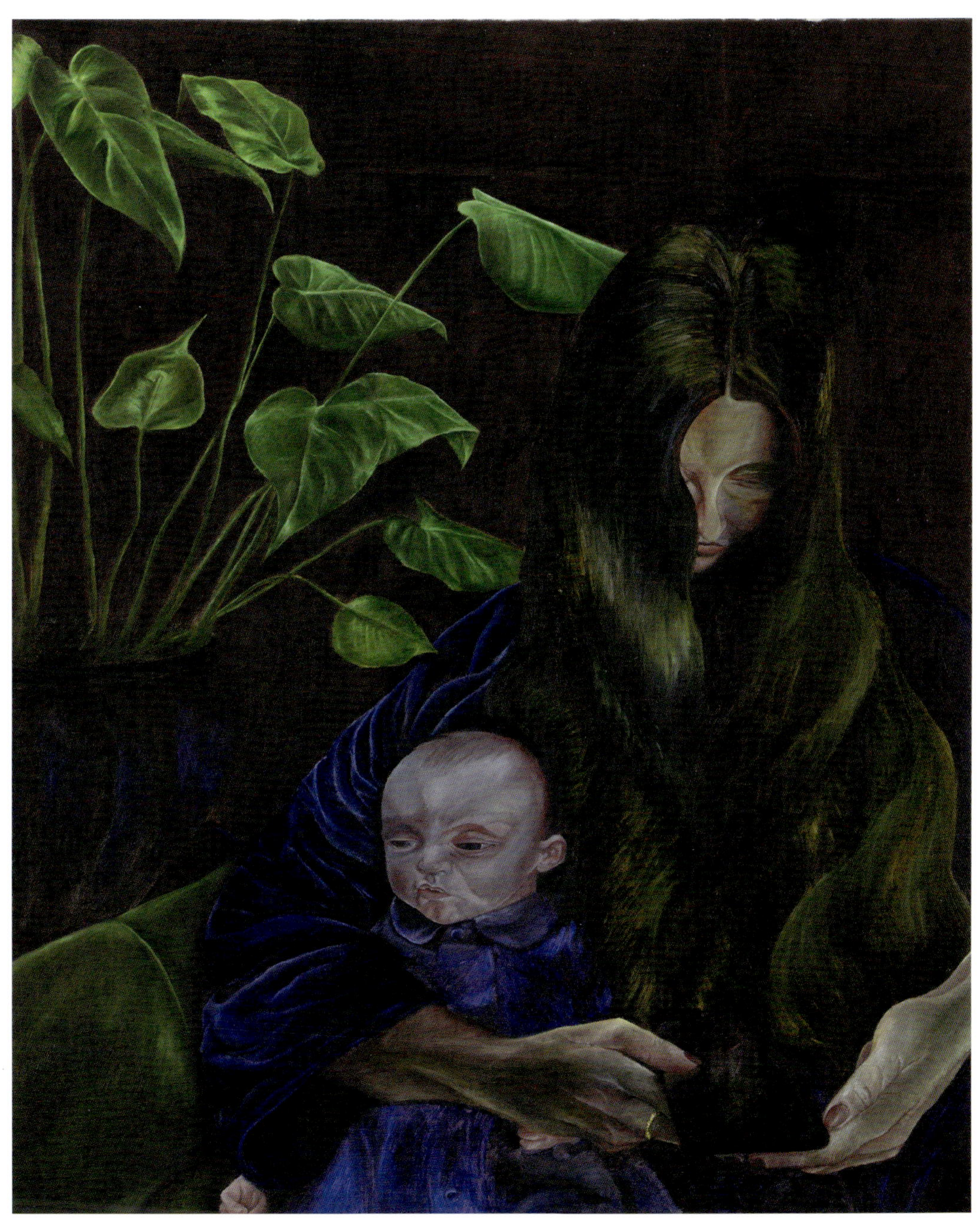

Mother and Child, 2018. Oil on linen. 30 × 24 in. Private collection. Photo: Aurélien Mole

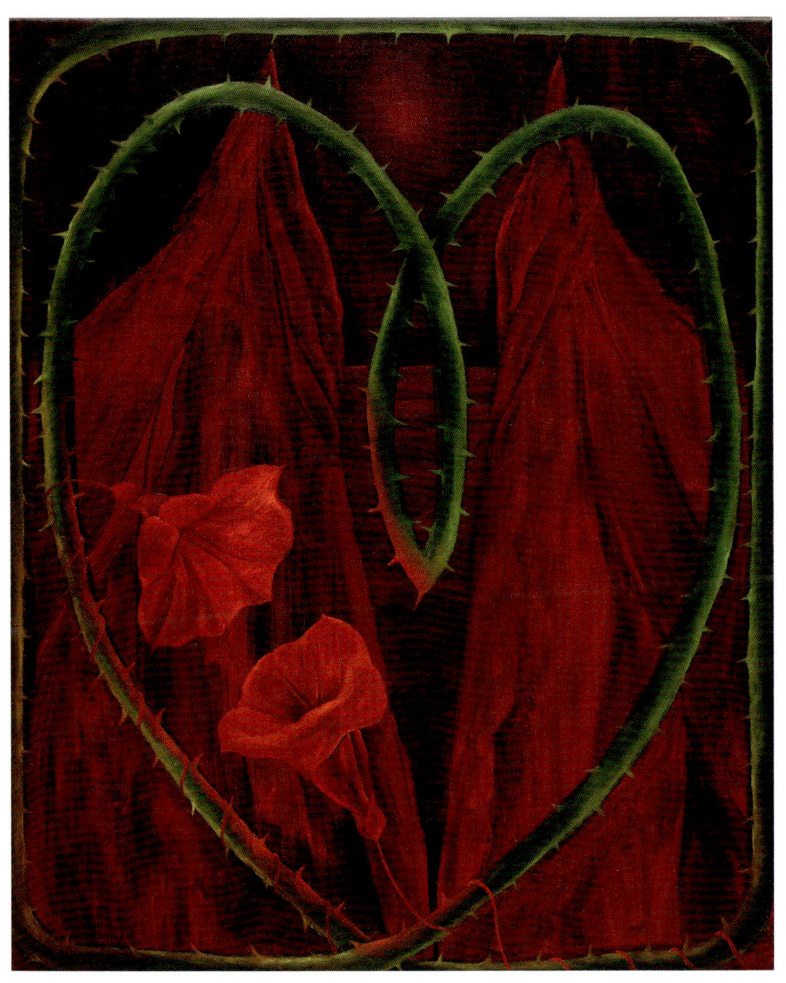

Twin Peaks, 2019. Oil on canvas. 20 × 16 in. Private collection. Photo: Charles Benton

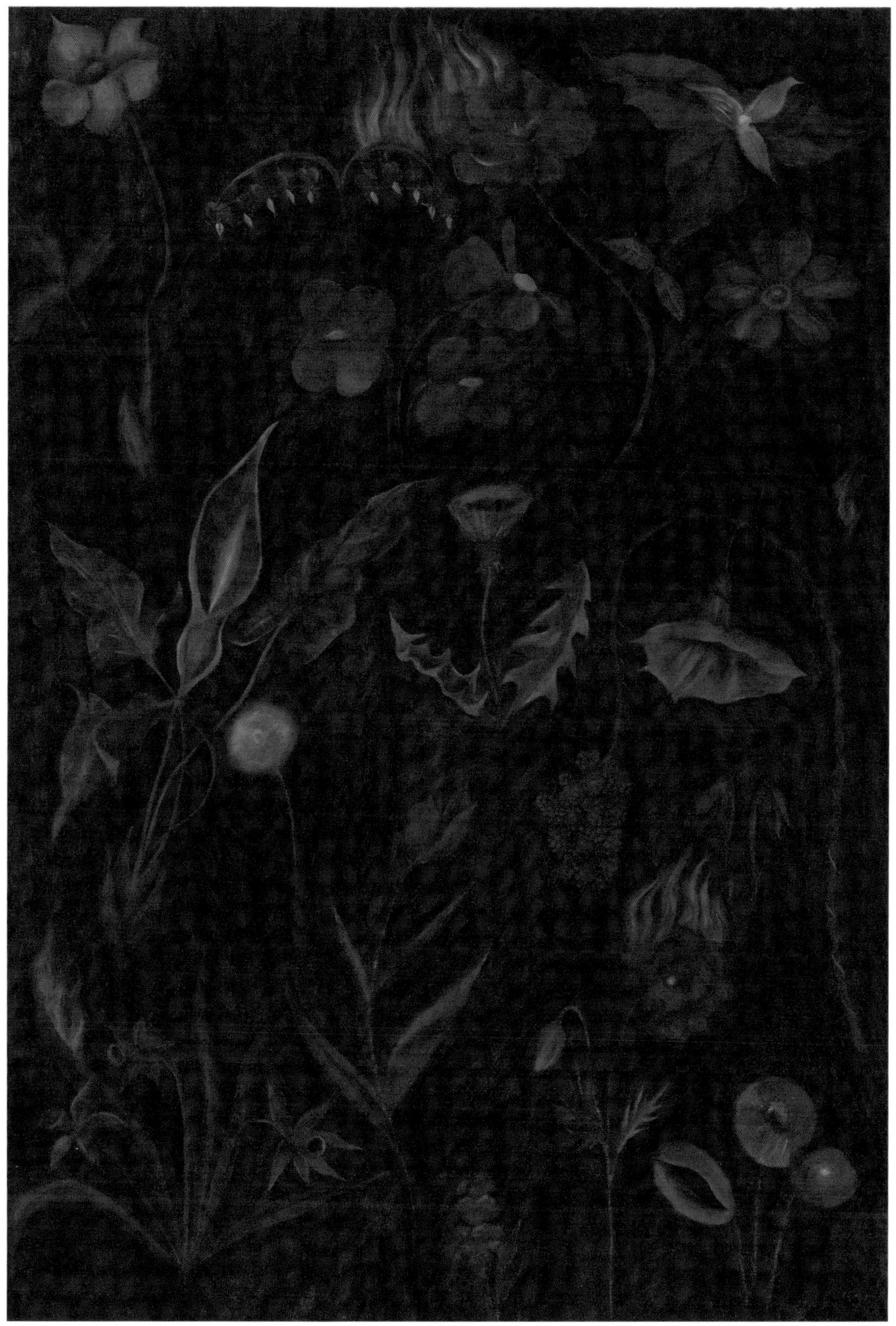

Flowers on Fire, 2019. Oil on canvas. 36 × 24 in. Private collection. Photo: Mario Gallucci

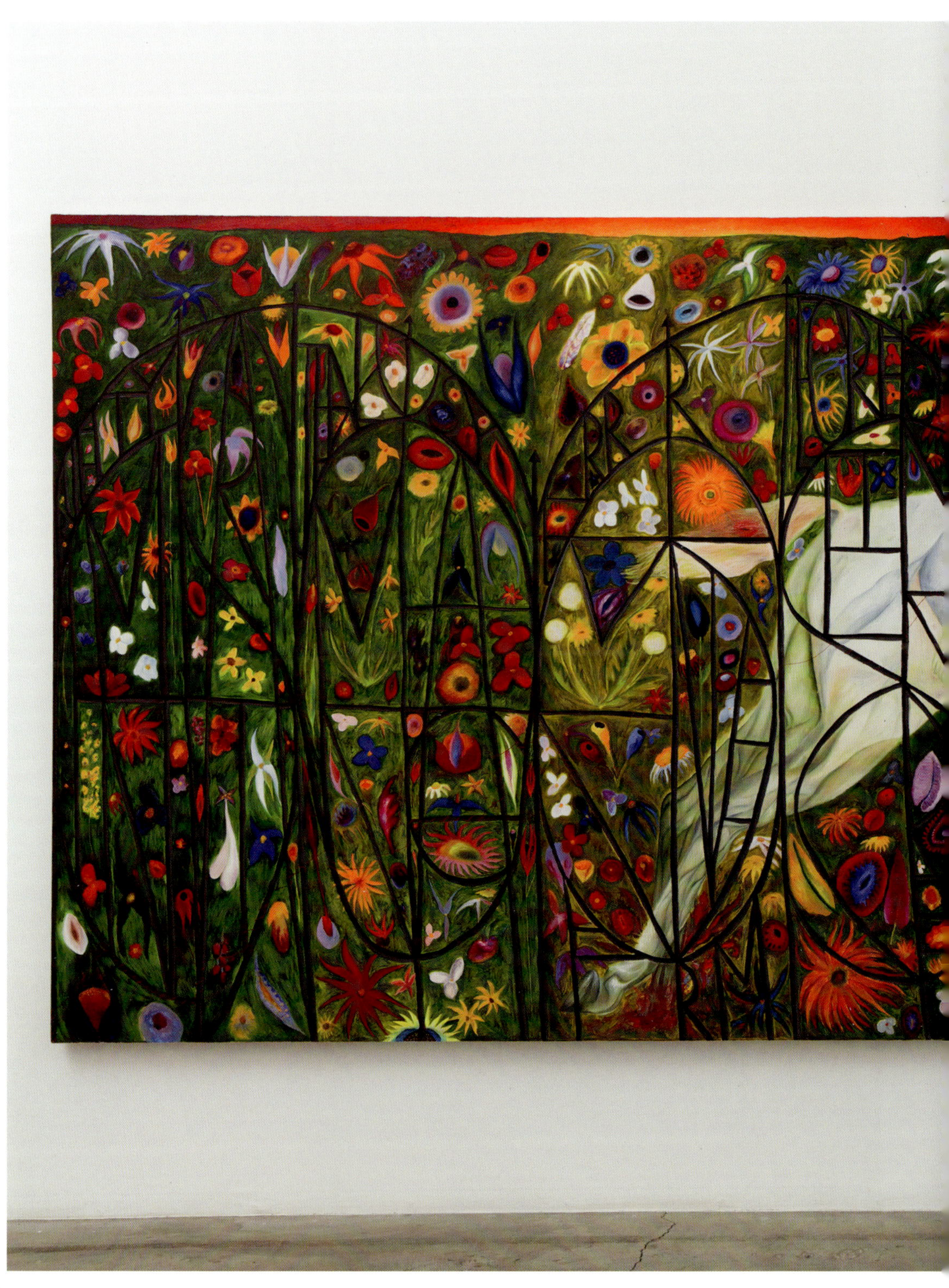

Pale Rider, 2019. Oil on canvas. 84 × 192 in. Collection of Lara and Jeff Sanderson. Photo: Michael Underwood

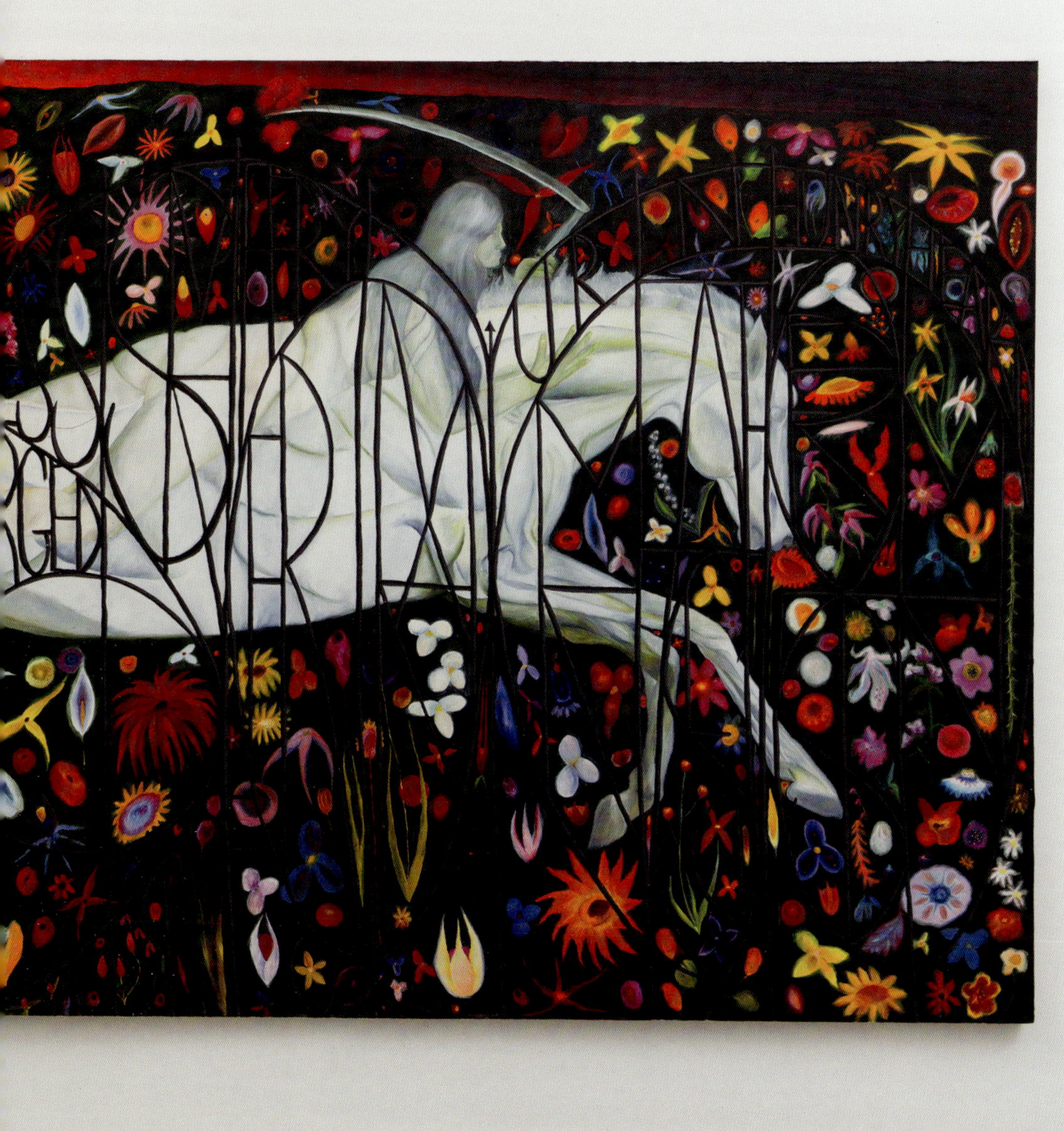

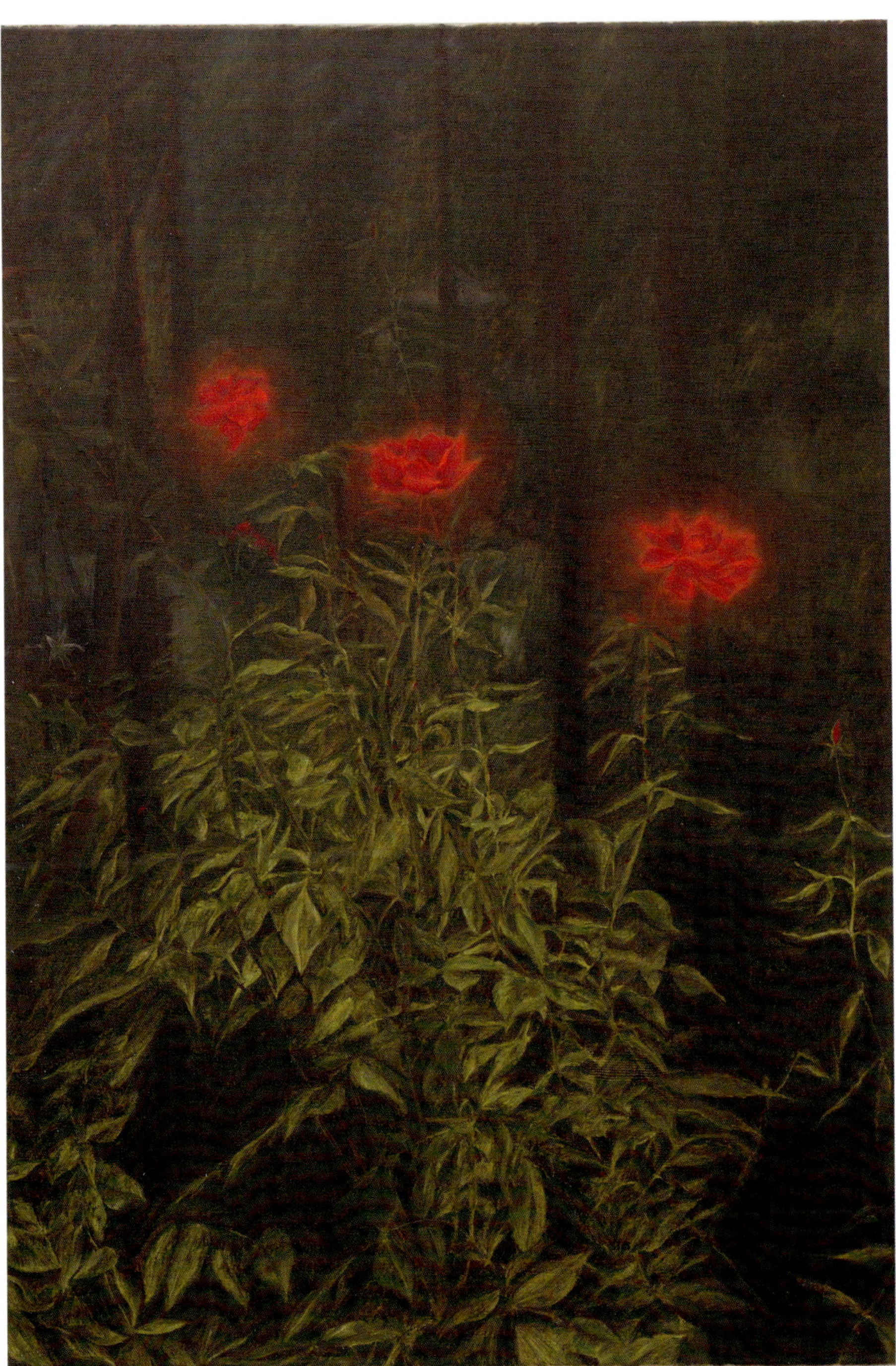

Roselight, 2019. Oil on linen. 36 × 24 in. Private collection. Photo: Mario Gallucci

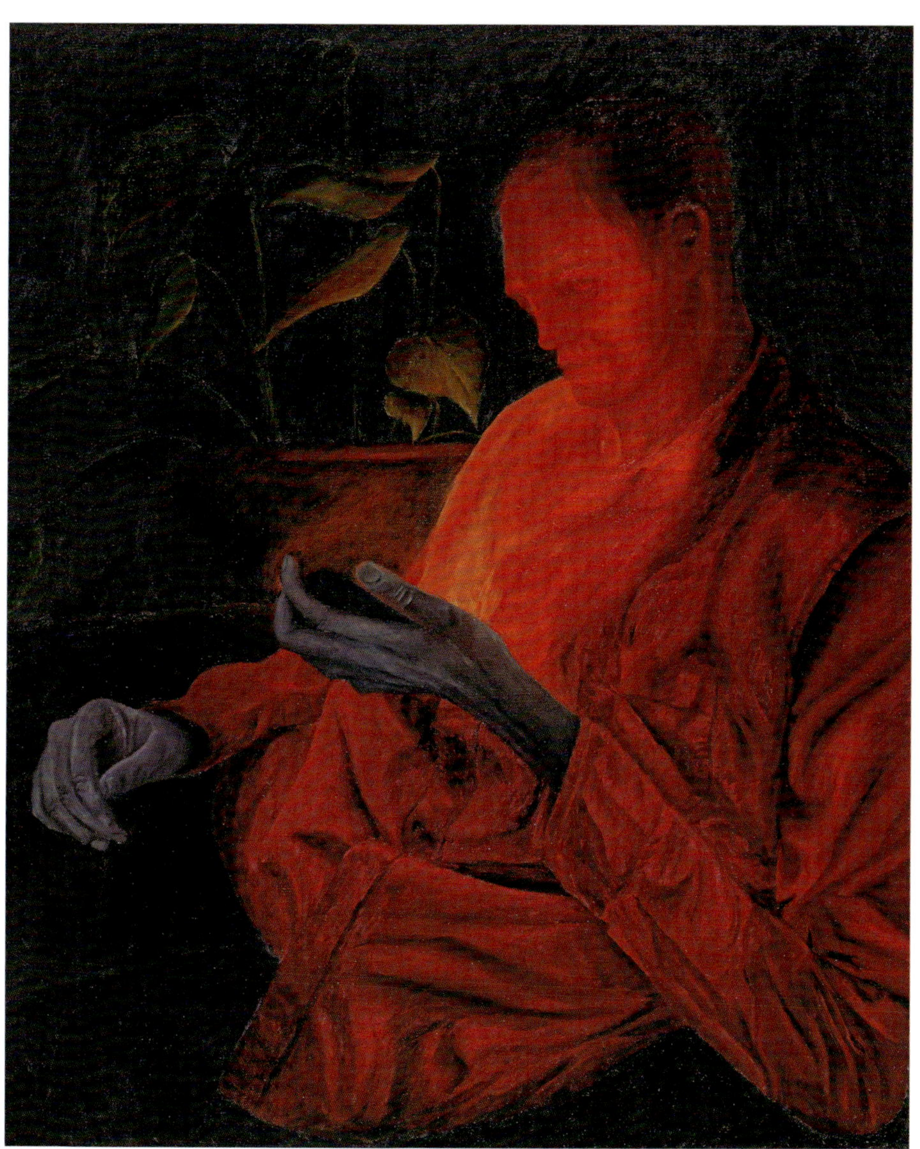

Alizarin shirt, 2019. Oil on linen. 30 × 24 in. Private collection. Photo: Mario Gallucci

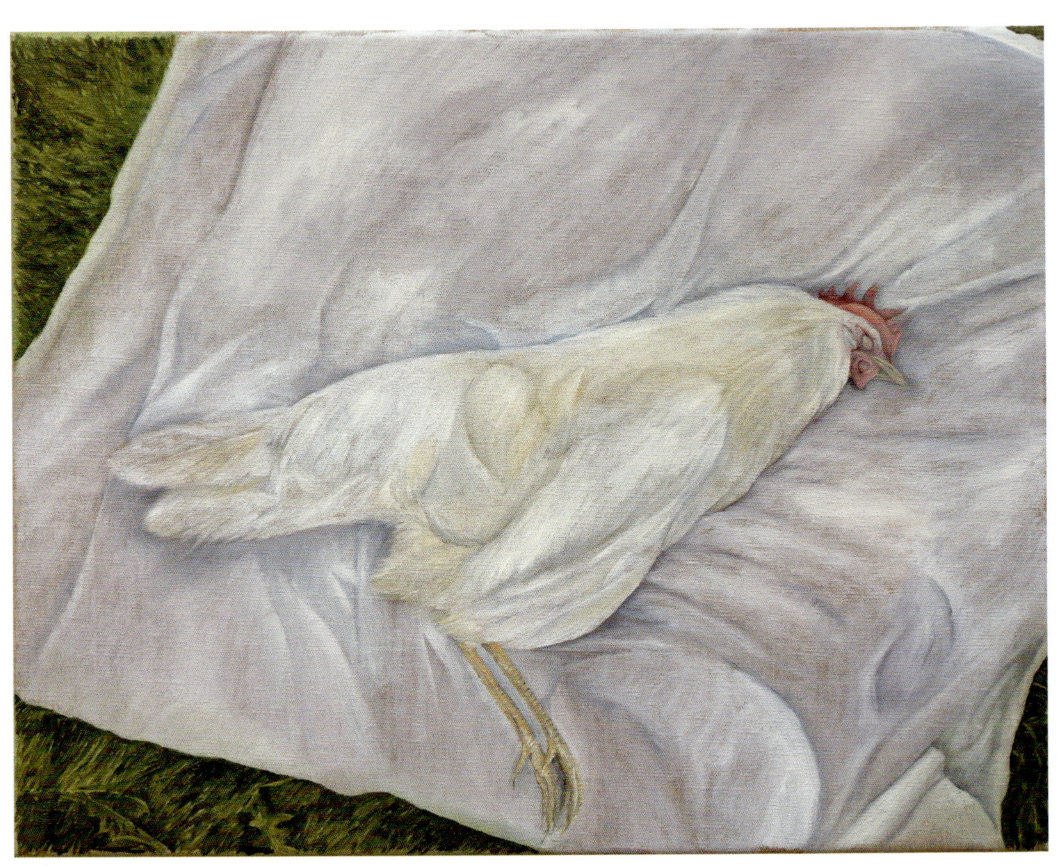

Valentine before her burial, 2020. Oil on linen. 16 × 20 in. Courtesy of Foxy Production, New York. Photo: Charles Benton

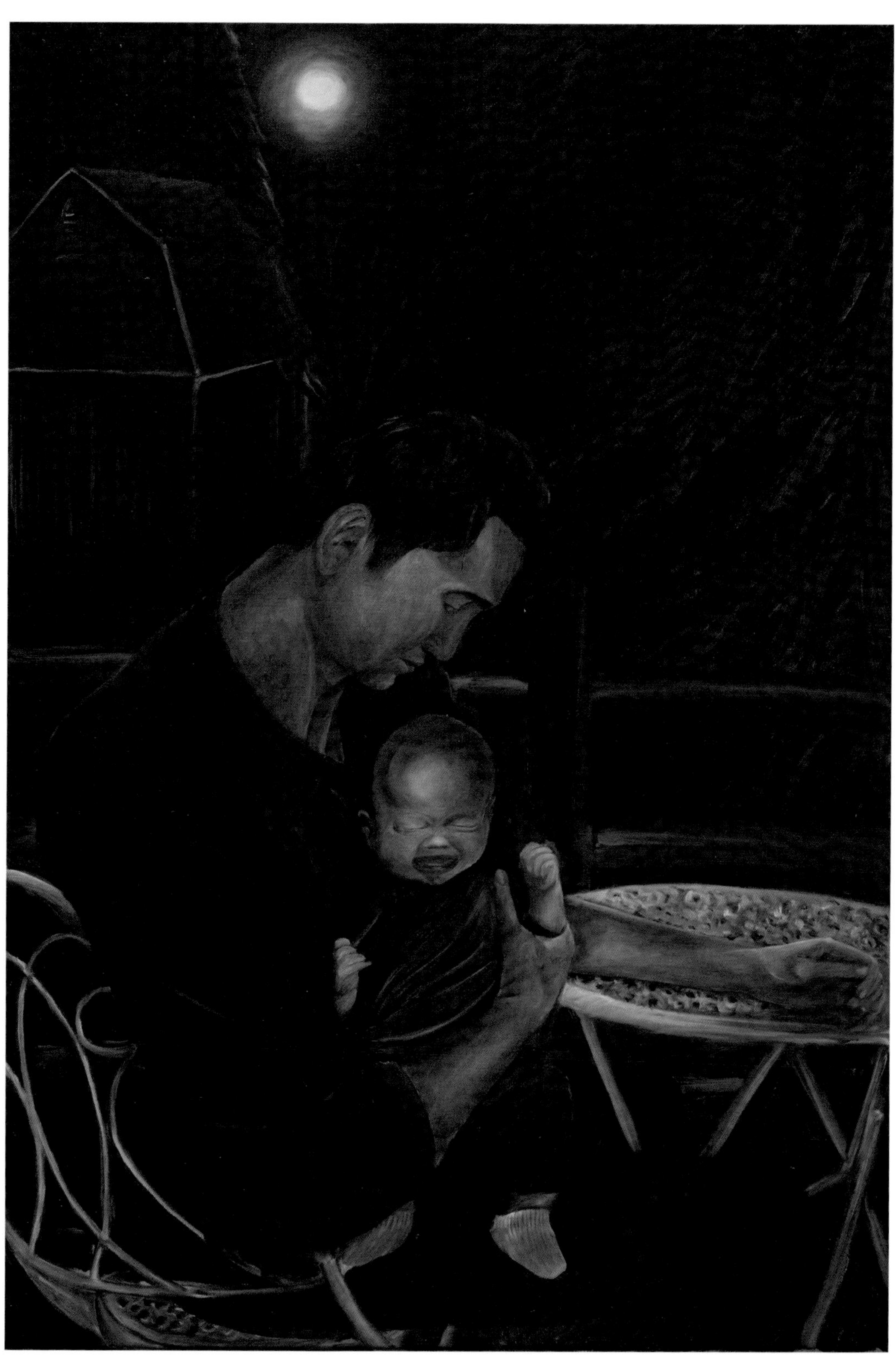

Father and Son, 2020. Oil on linen. 36 × 24 in. Courtesy of Foxy Production, New York.
Photo: Charles Benton

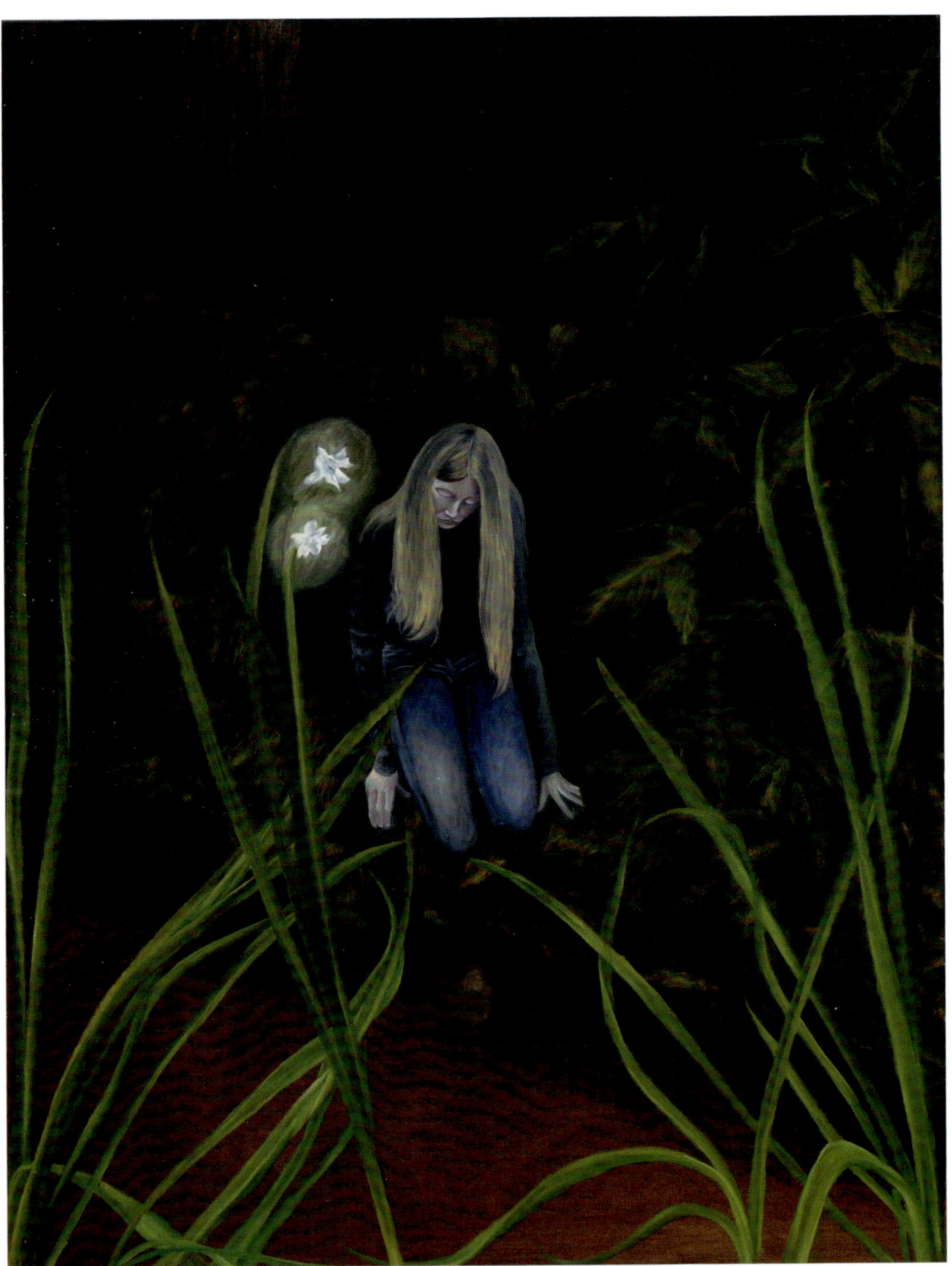

Narcissus, 2020. Oil on linen. 40 × 30 in. Private collection. Photo: Charles Benton

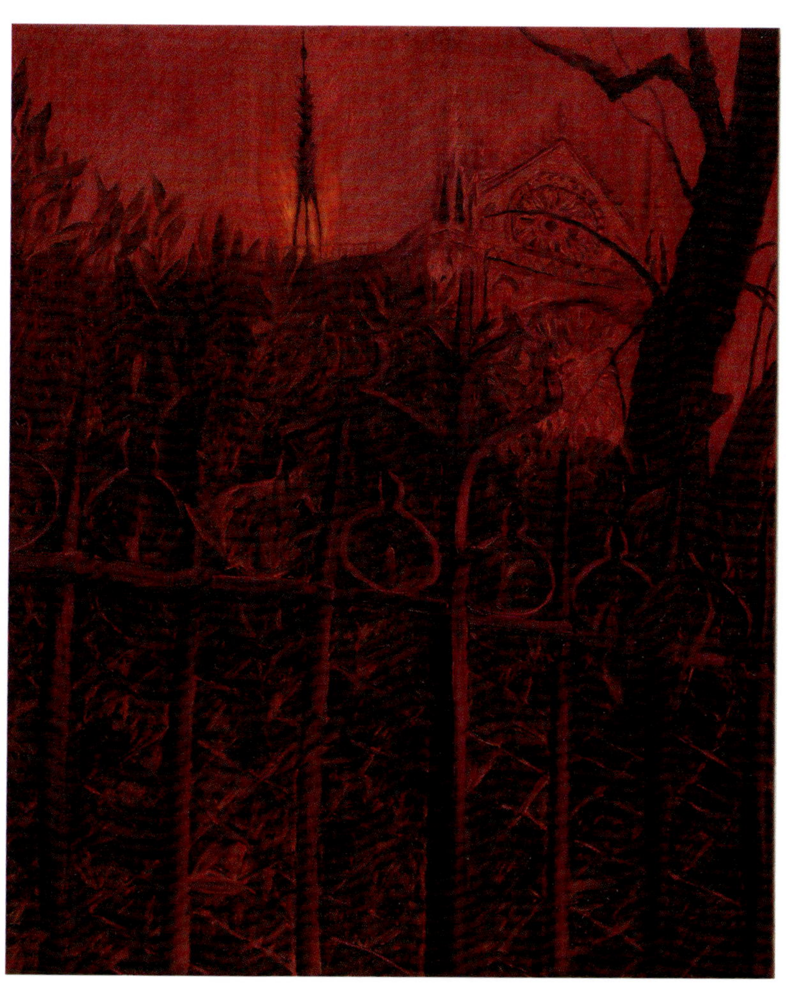

Notre Dame on Fire, 2020. Oil on linen. 20 × 16 in. Private collection. Photo: Charles Benton

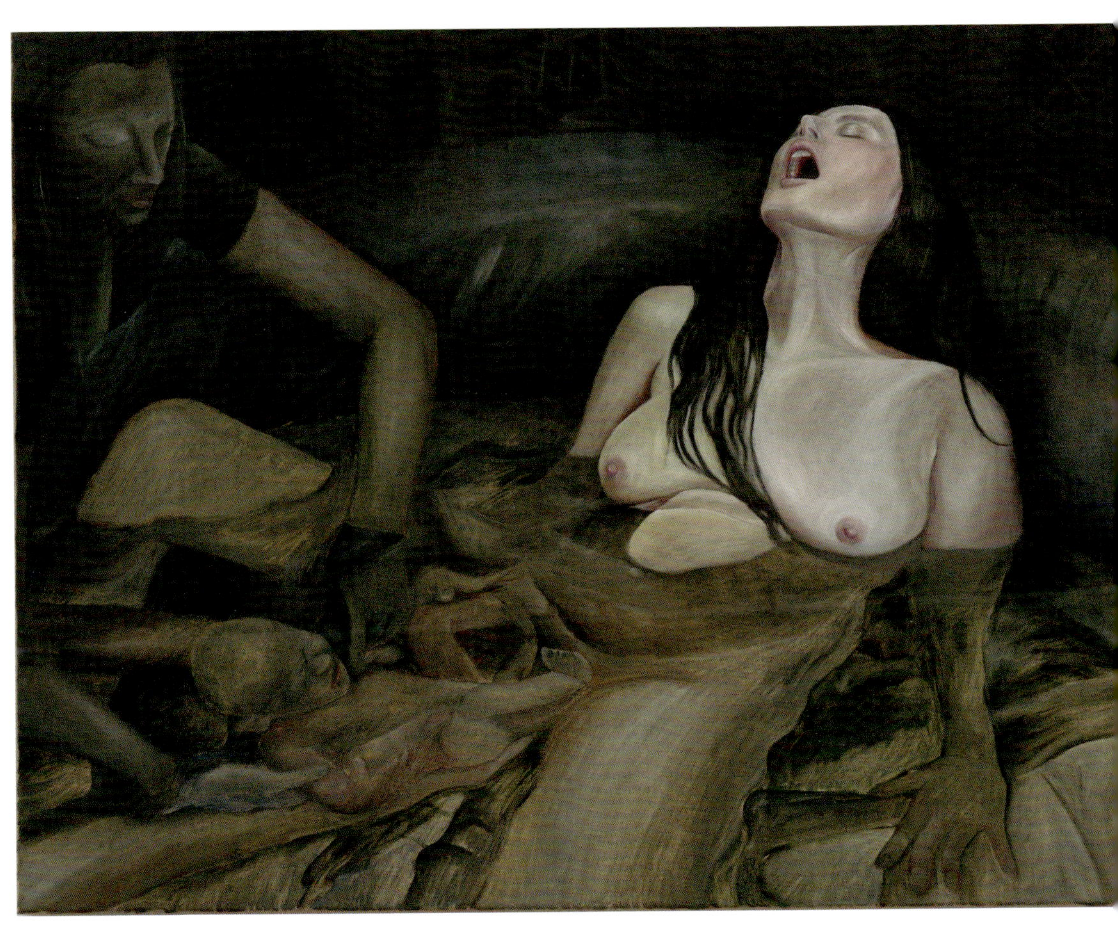

Birth, 2019. Oil on linen. 24 × 36 in. Private collection. Photo: Michael Underwood

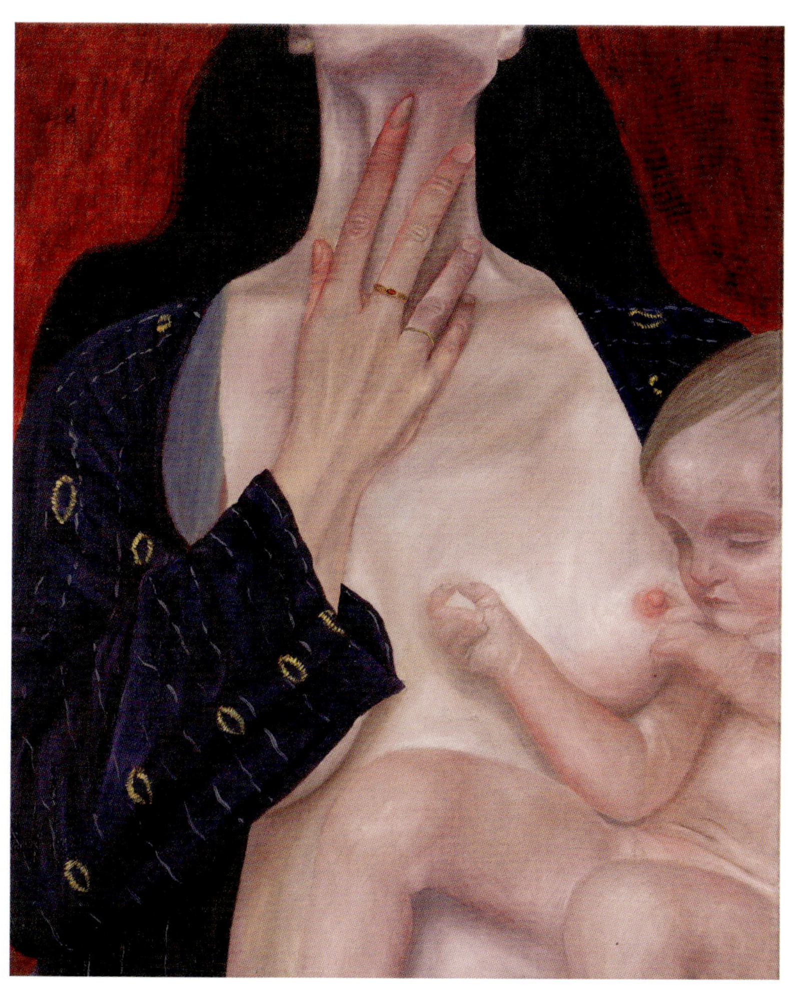

Mother and Child, 2019. Oil on linen. 20 × 16 in. Private collection. Photo: Mario Gallucci

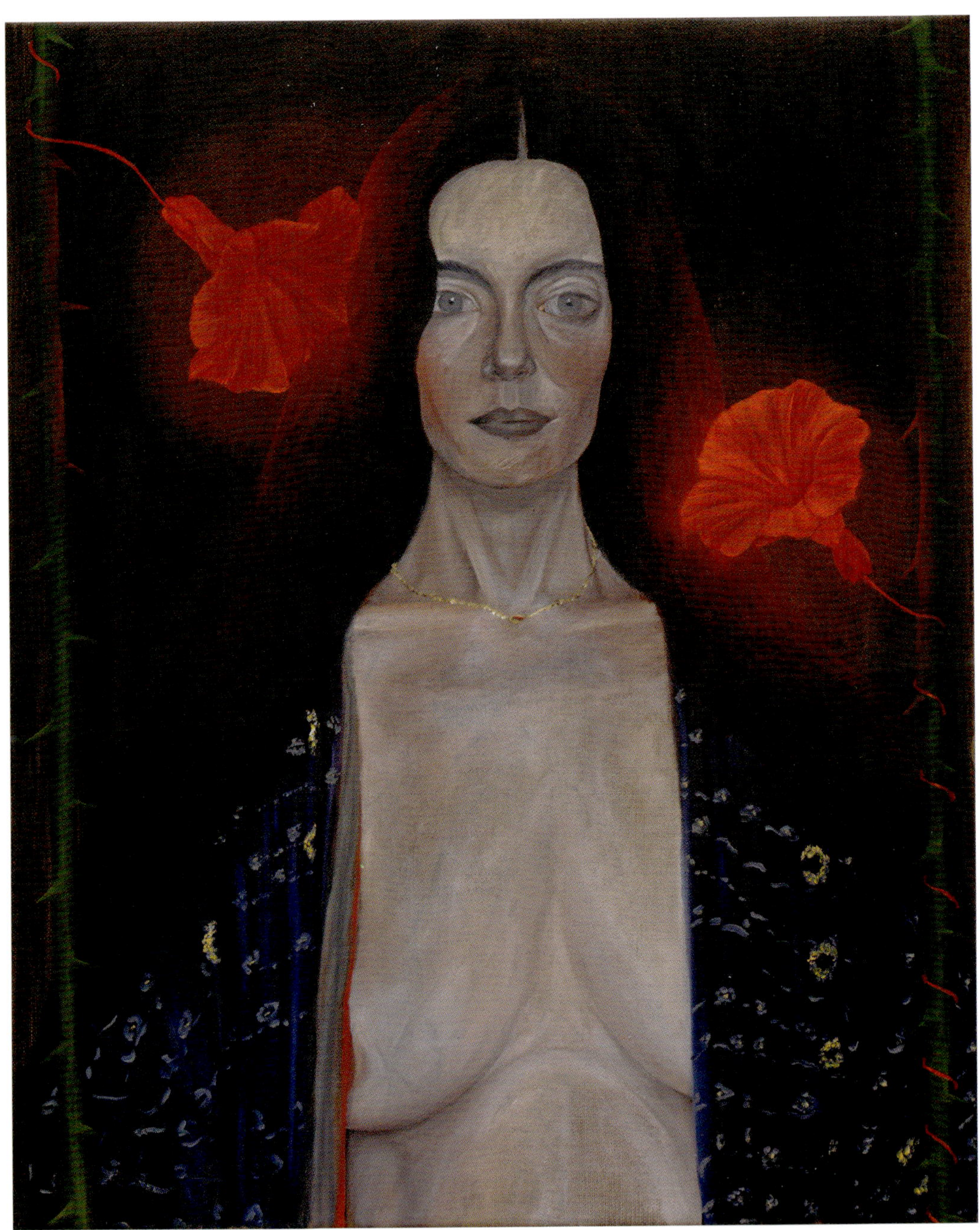

 With Child, 2020. Oil on linen. 20 × 16 in. Private collection. Photo: Charles Benton

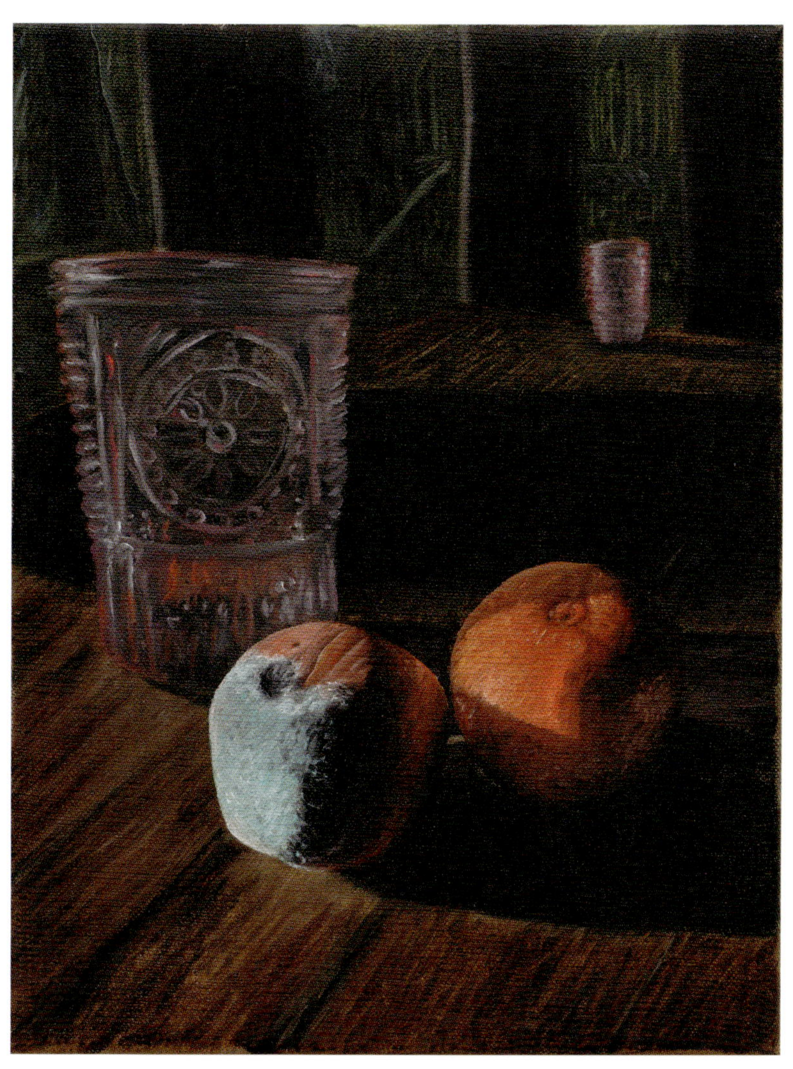

Two Clementines, 2020. Oil on linen. 12 × 9 in. Private collection. Photo: Charles Benton

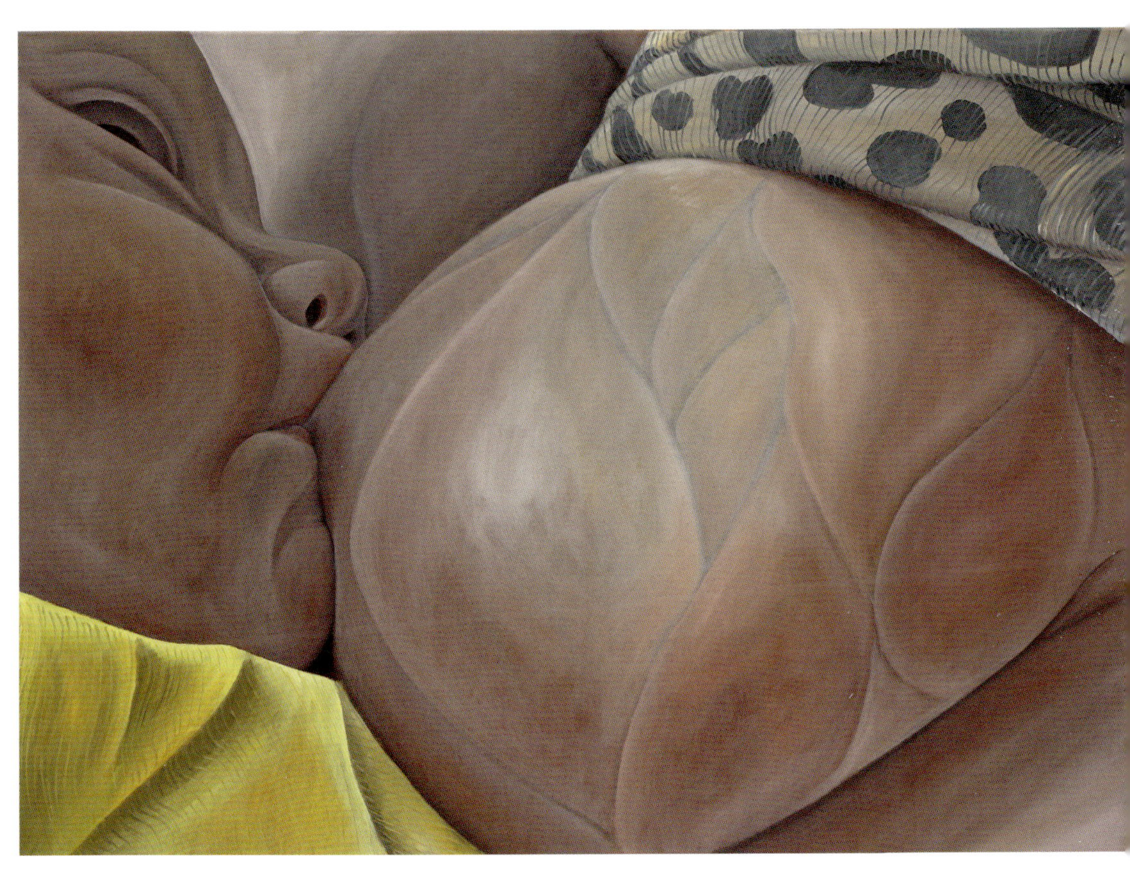

Mother and Child, 2019. Oil on linen. 30 × 40 in. Courtesy of Foxy Production, New York.
Photo: Charles Benton

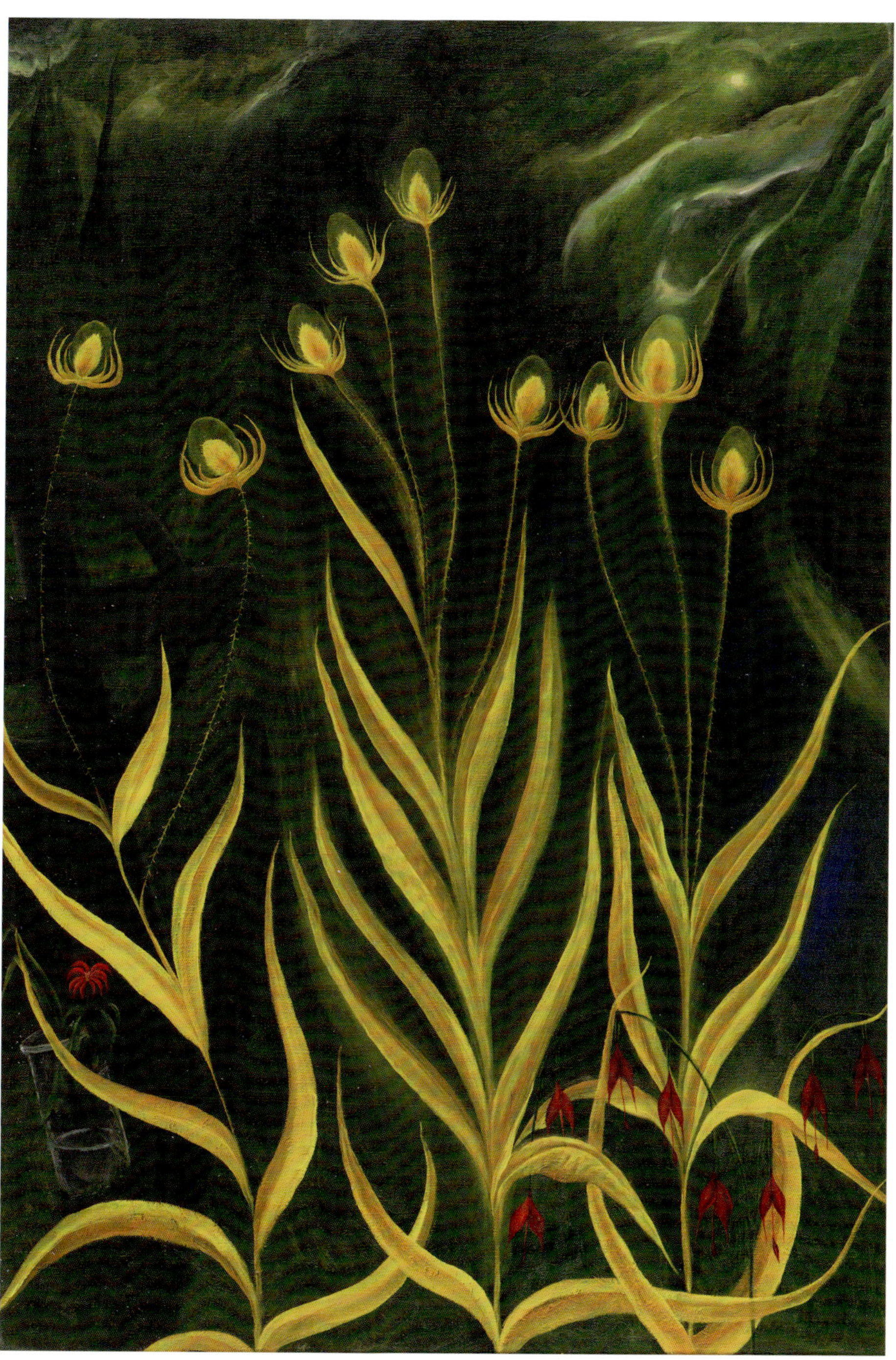

Memorial Day Thistle, 2021. Oil on linen. 36 × 24 in. Private collection. Photo: Charles Benton

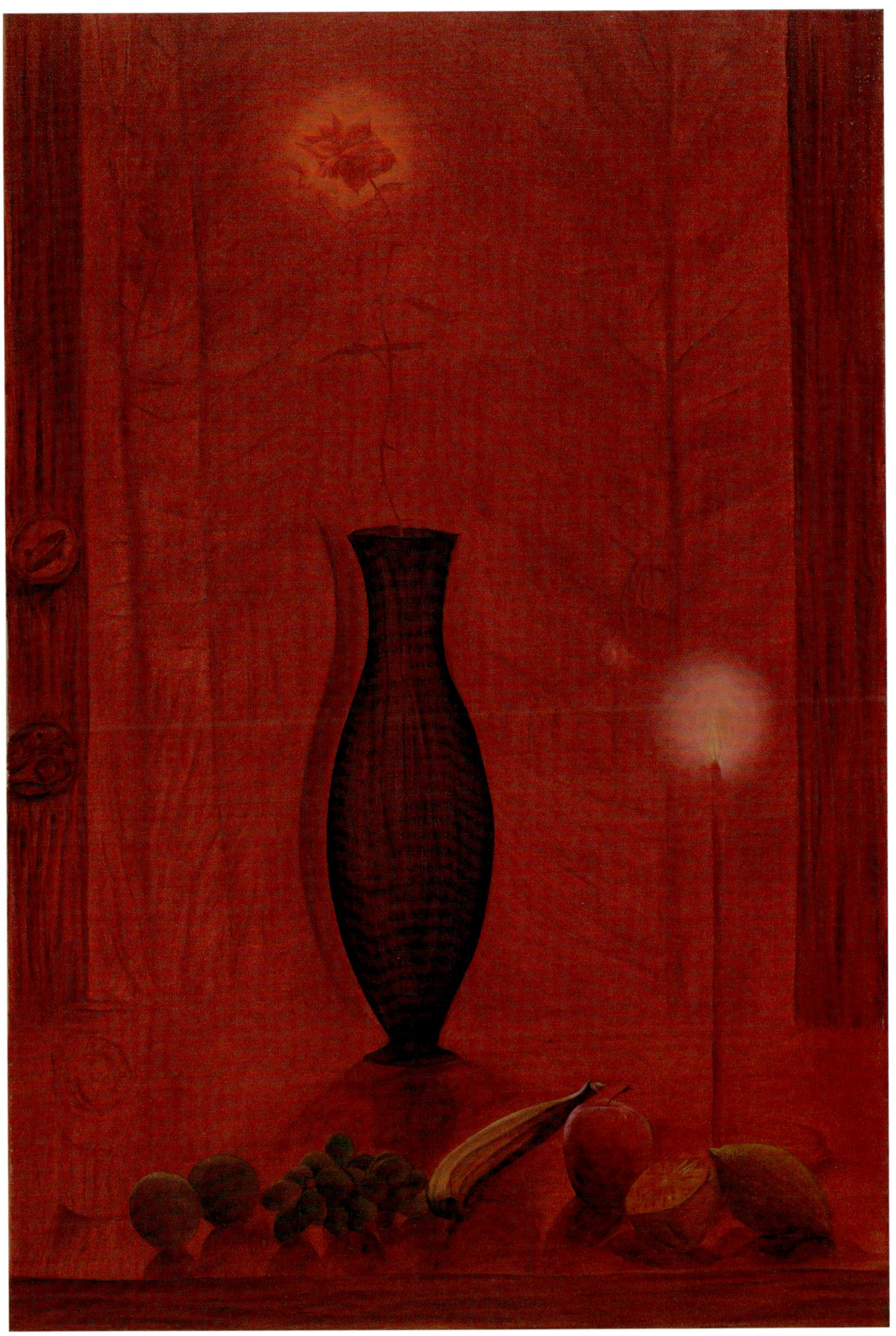

Winter Still Life, 2021. Oil on linen. 36 × 24 in. Private collection. Photo: Charles Benton

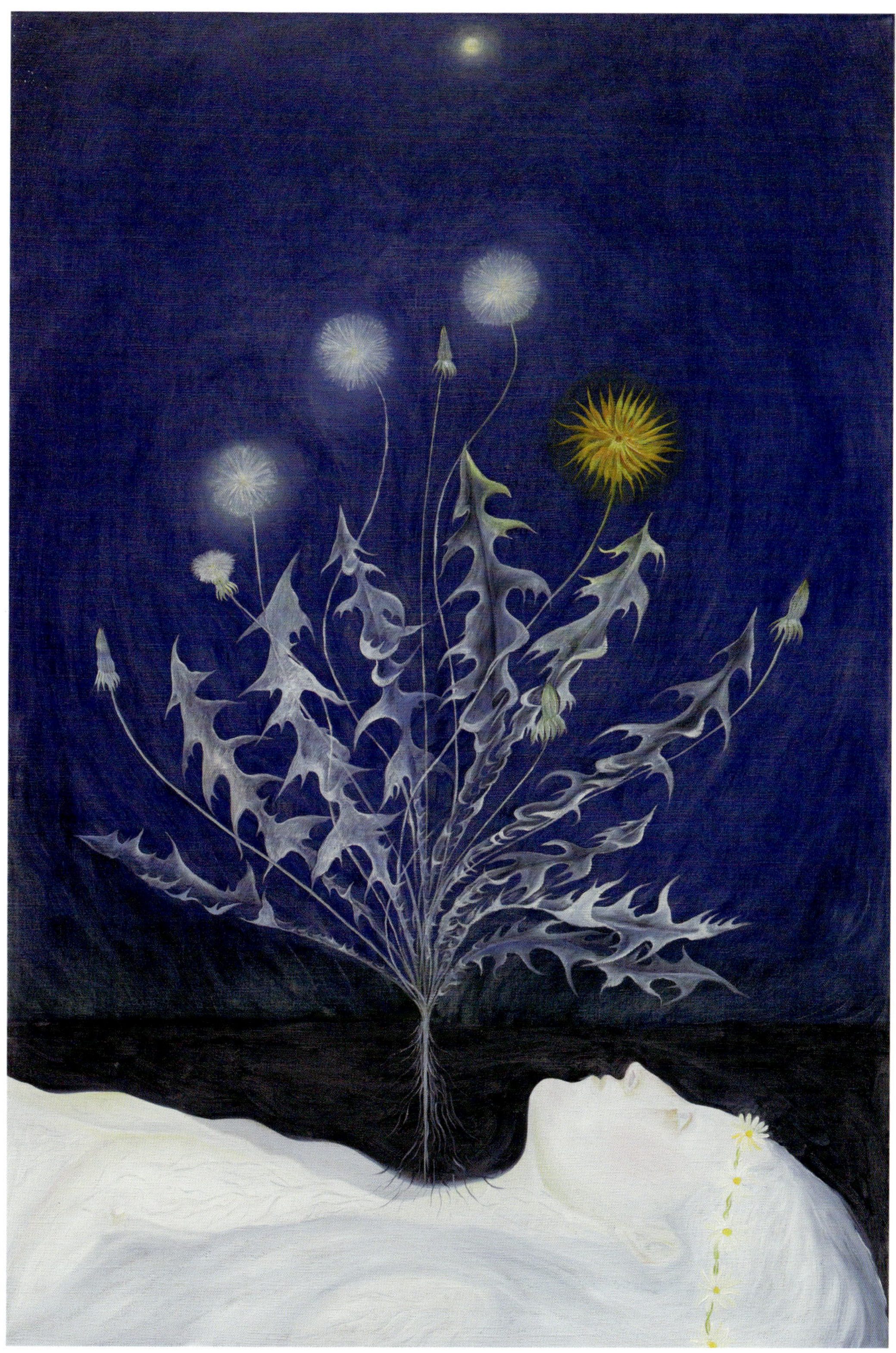

Dandelion Song, 2021. Oil on linen. 36 × 24 in. Private collection. Photo: Charles Benton

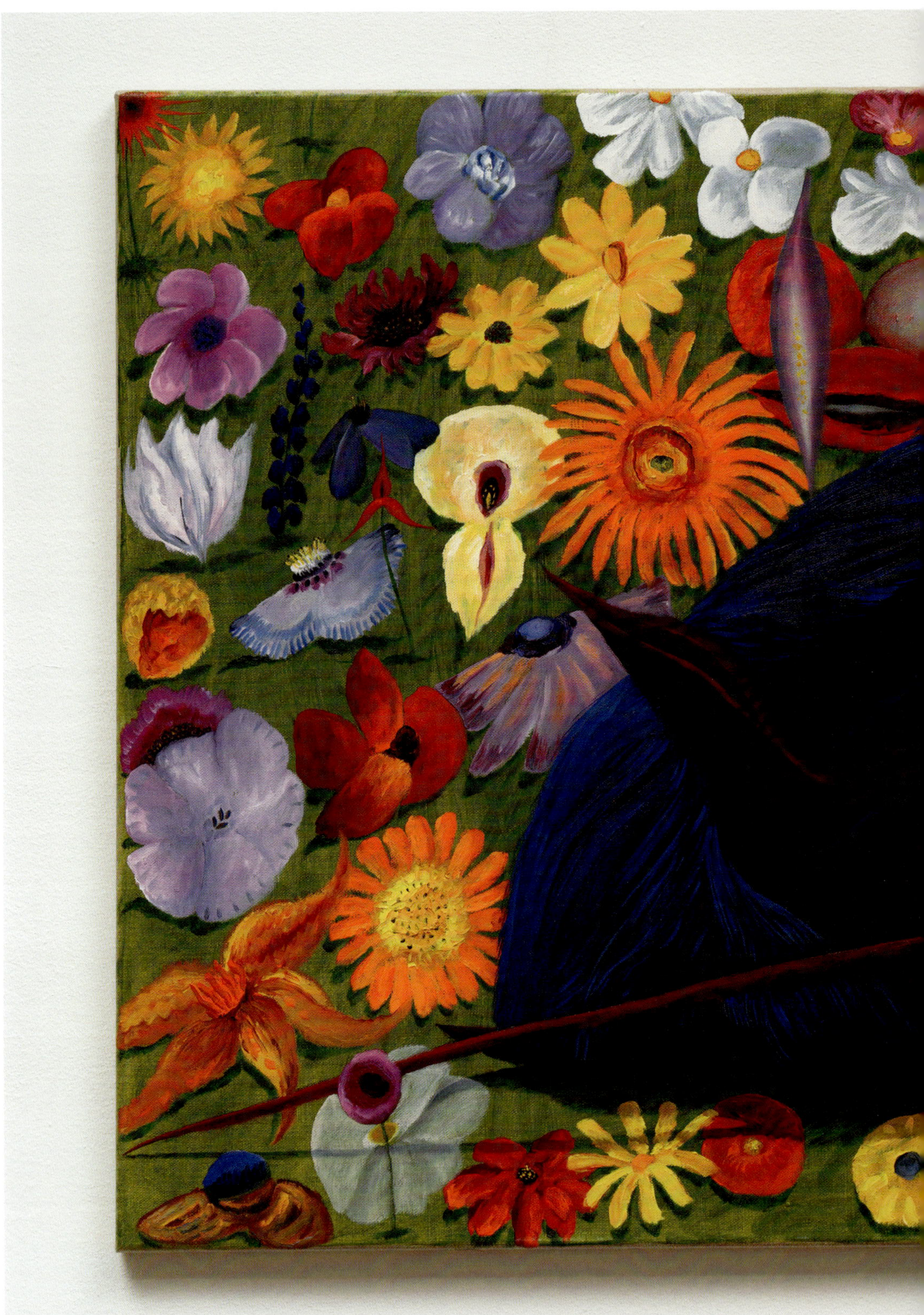

Unicorn Dreaming, 2021. Oil on linen. 24 × 36 in. Private collection. Photo: Charles Benton

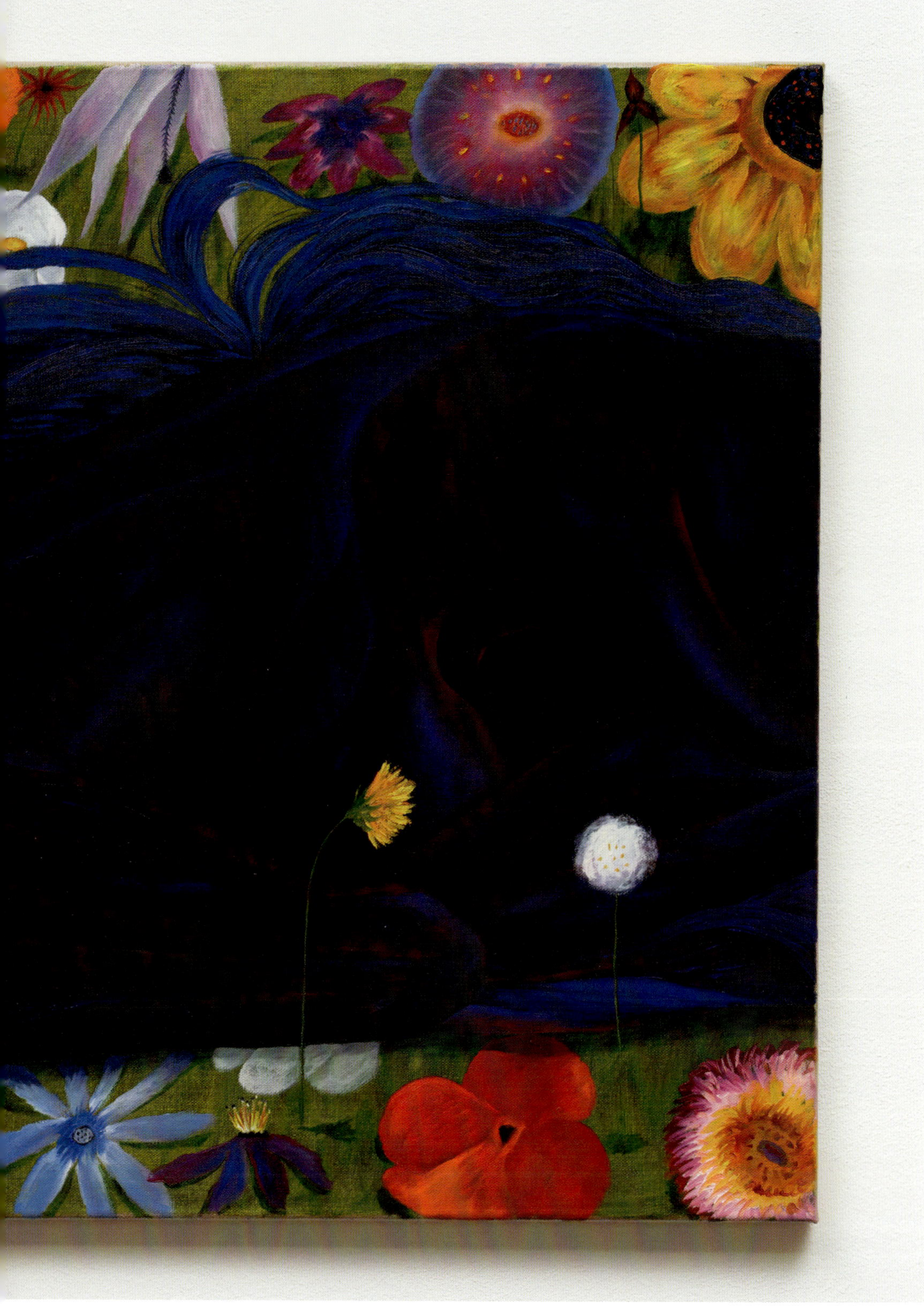

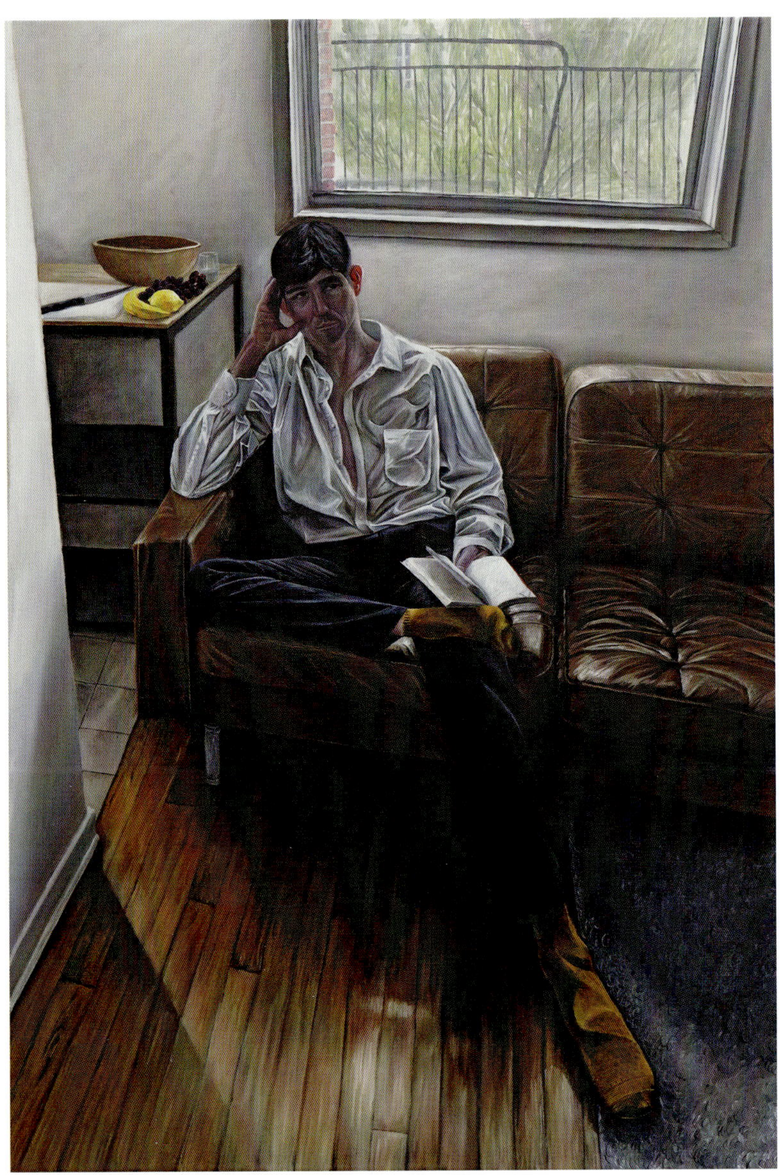

The Writer, 2021. Oil on linen. 36 × 24 in. Private collection. Photo: Aurélien Mole

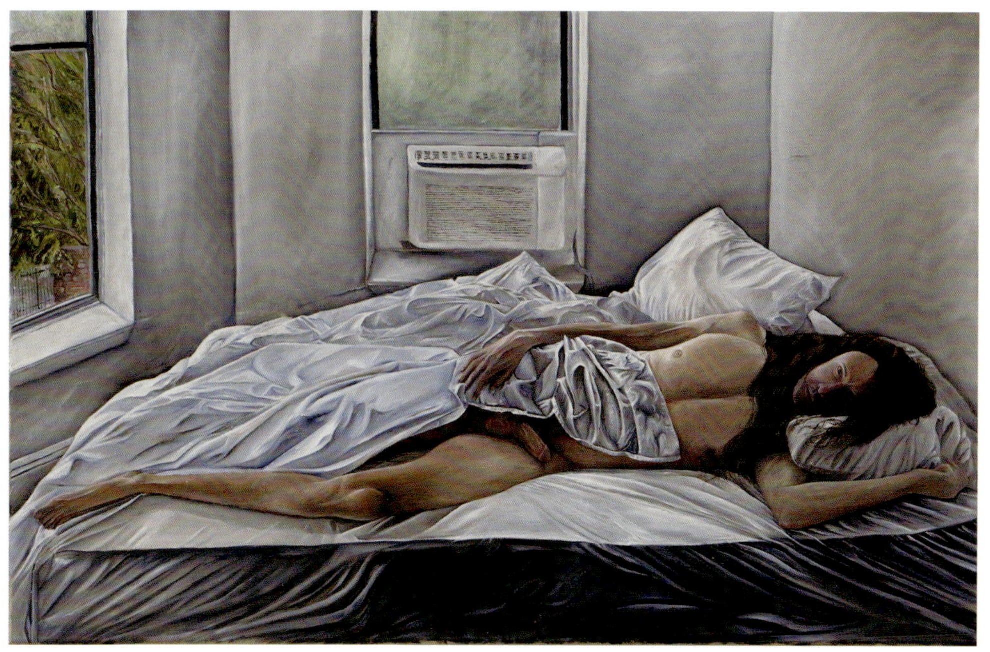

The Comedian, 2021. Oil on linen. 24 × 36 in. Private collection. Photo: Aurélien Mole

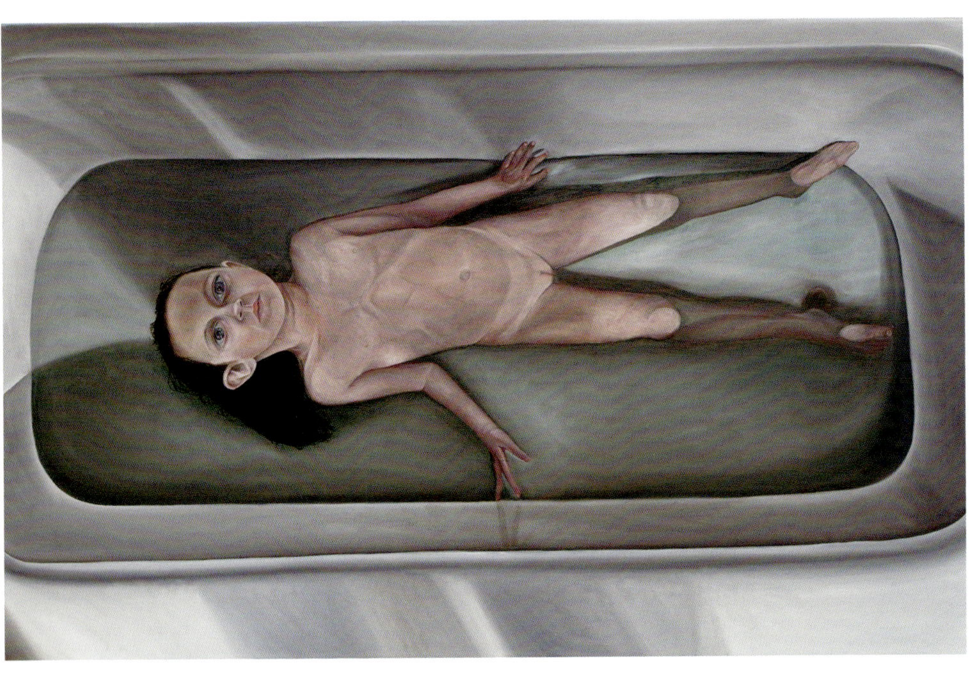

The Future, 2021. Oil on linen. 24 × 36 in. Private collection. Photo: Aurélien Mole

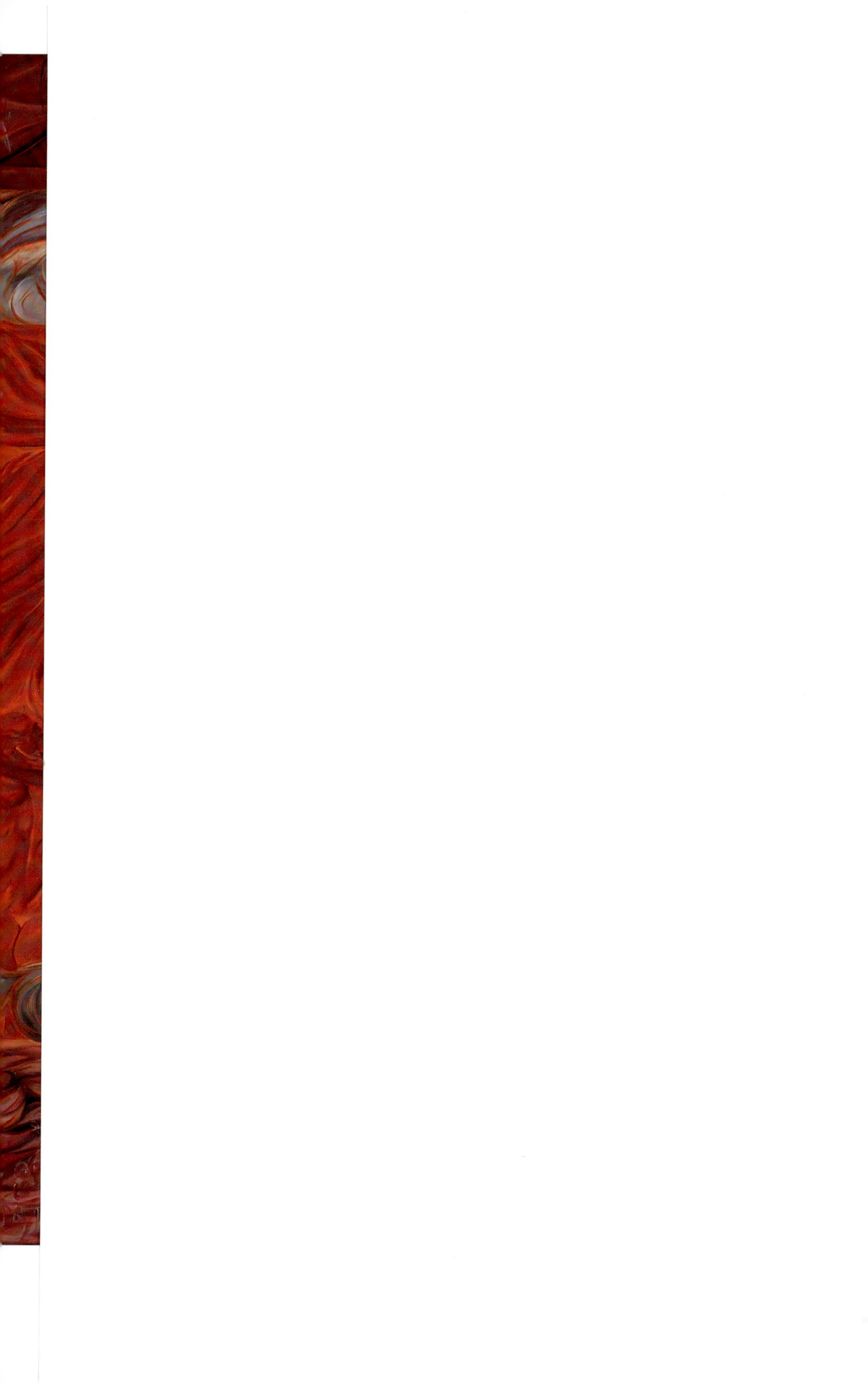

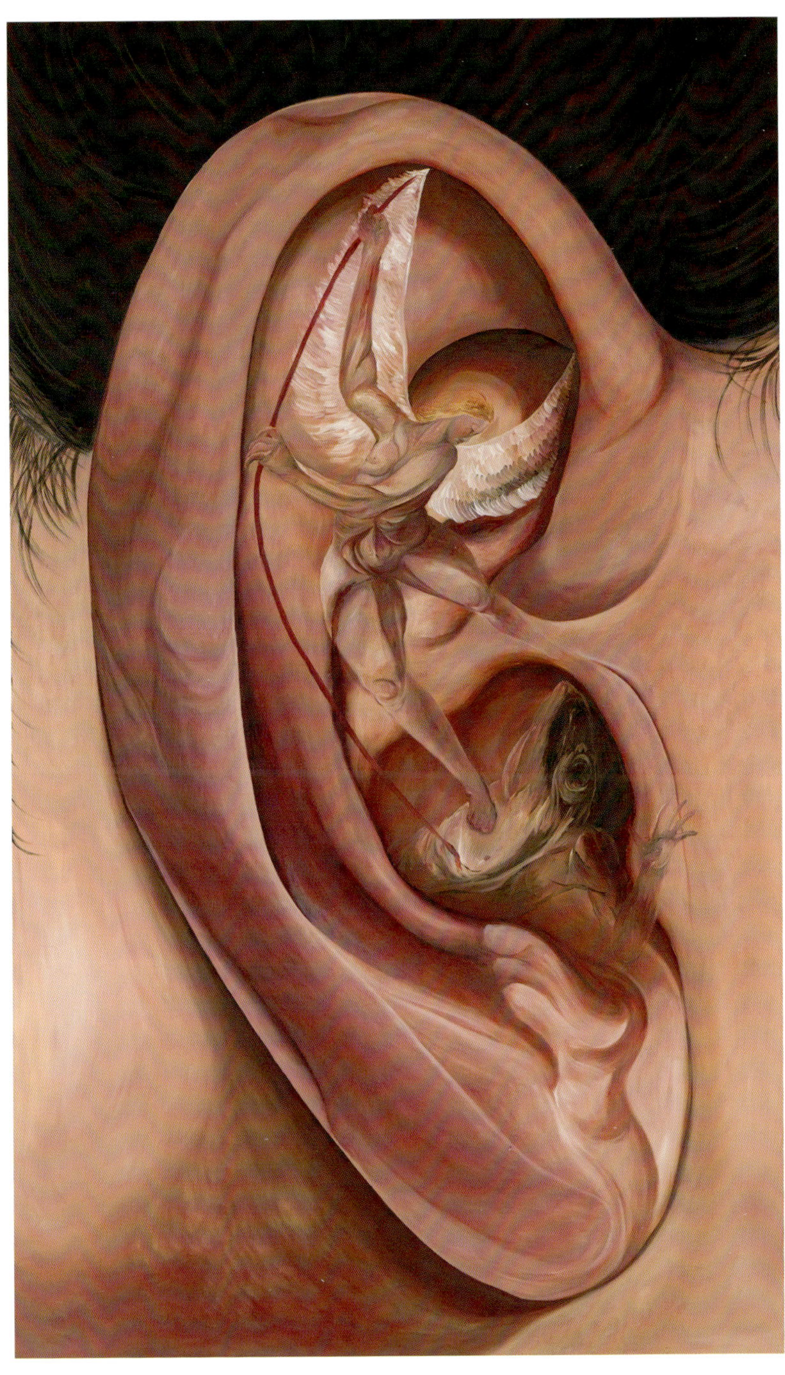

Ear (Good), 2022. Oil on canvas. 126 × 72 in. Courtesy of Ciaccia Levi, Paris-Milan, and Foxy Production, New York. Photo: Mario Gallucci

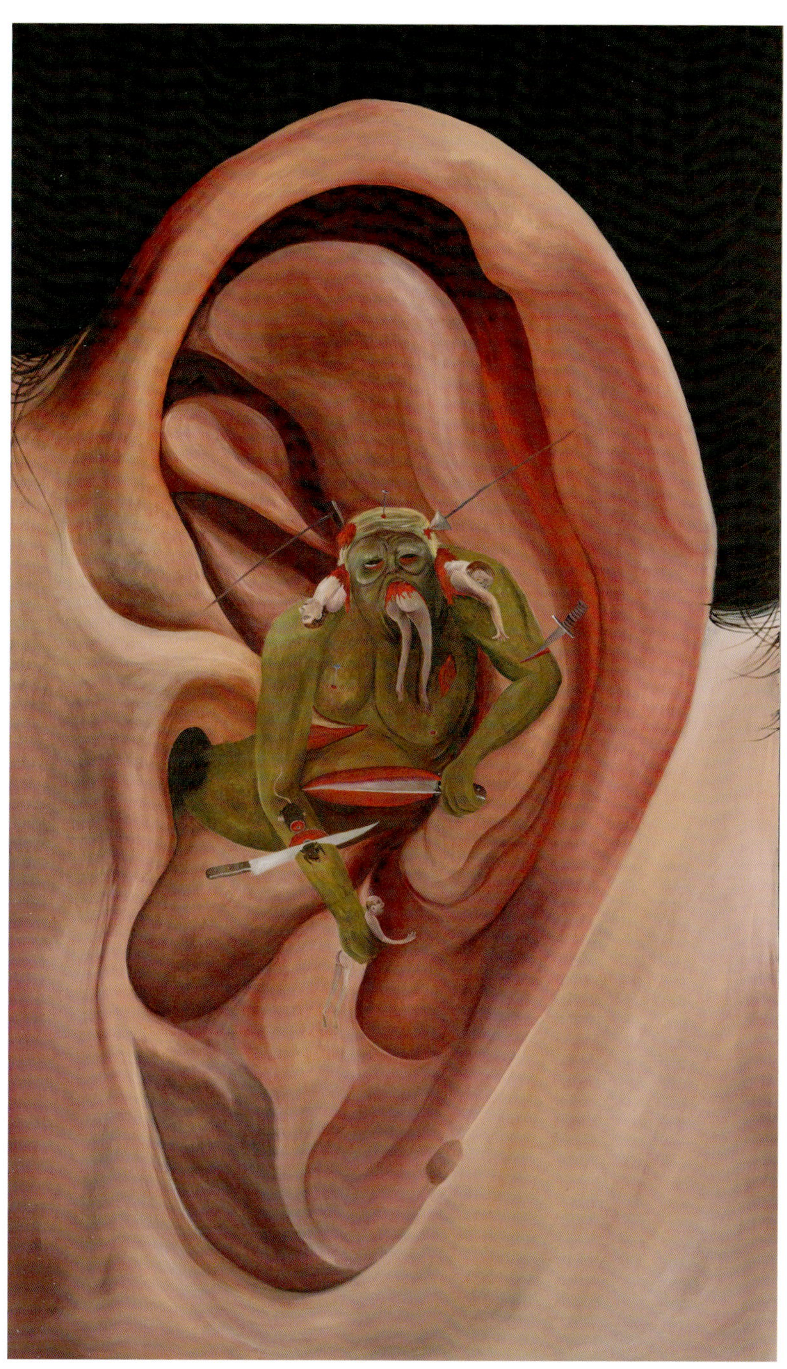

Ear (Bad), 2022. Oil on linen. 126 × 72 in. Courtesy of Ciaccia Levi, Paris-Milan, and Foxy Production, New York. Photo: Mario Gallucci

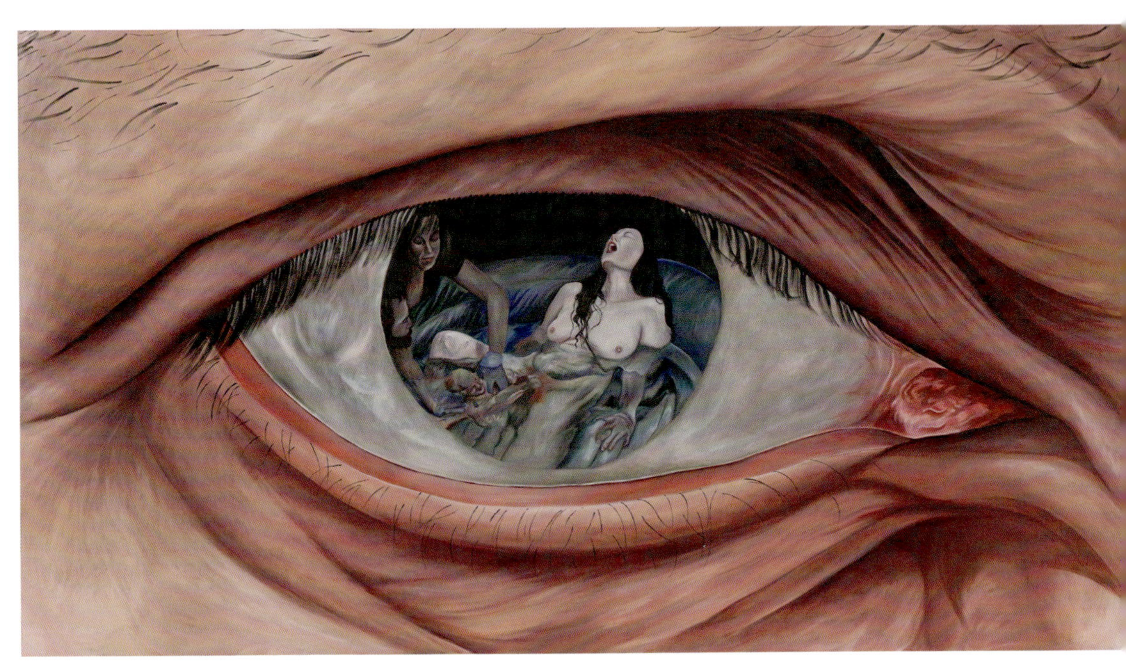

Eye (Birth), 2022. Oil on linen. 72 × 126 in. Courtesy of Ciaccia Levi, Paris-Milan, and Foxy Production, New York. Photo: Mario Gallucci

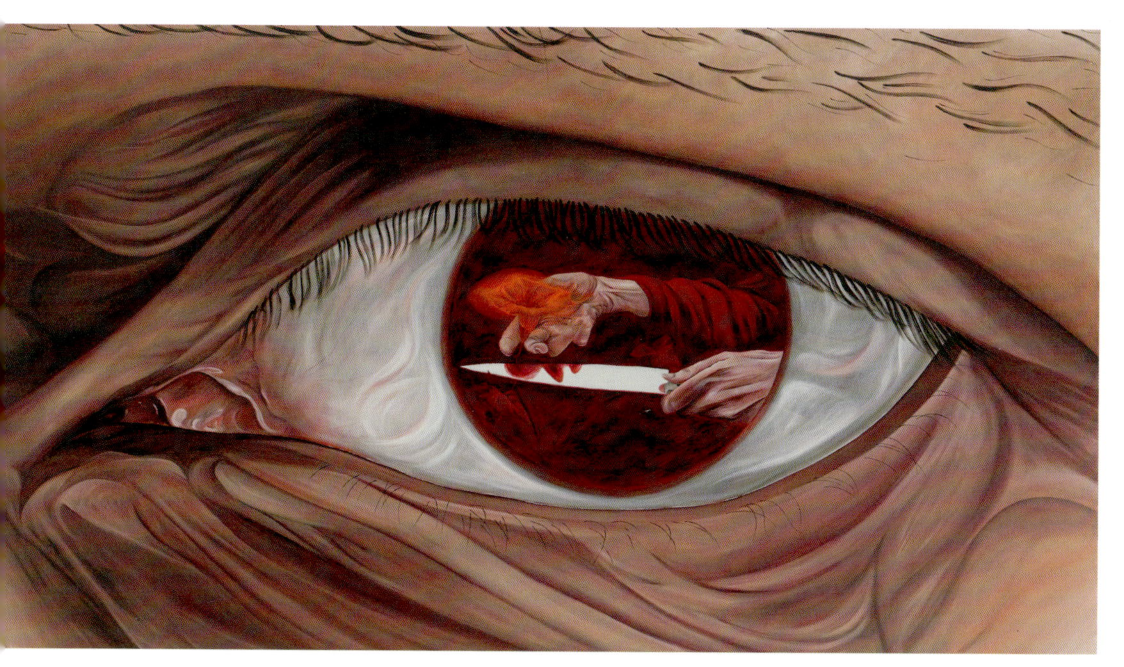

Eye (Morning Glory), 2022. Oil on linen. 72 × 126 in. Courtesy of Ciaccia Levi, Paris-Milan, and Foxy Production, New York. Photo: Mario Gallucci

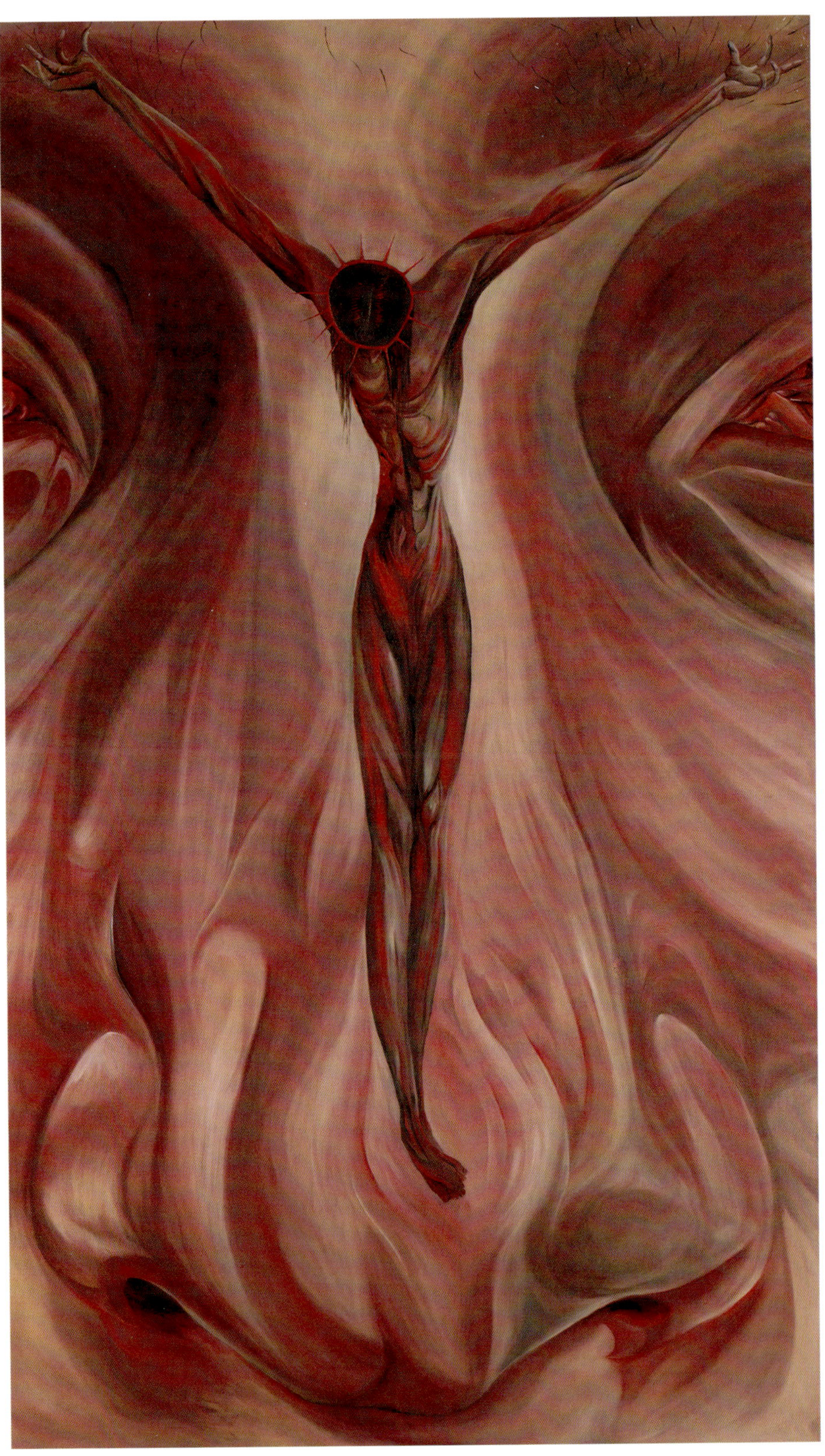

Nose (Crucifixion), 2022. Oil on linen. 126 × 72 in. Courtesy of Ciaccia Levi, Paris-Milan, and Foxy Production, New York. Photo: Mario Gallucci

Notes

Introduction / Doors, Portals, Passageways

1. Alexandra Schamel, "'. . . une apparition surnaturelle': Window-motif and framing strategies in Mörike and Proust," *Au-delà* (issue 17, 2014). Accessed January 3, 2022, at https://journals.openedition.org/trans/964?lang=en#ftn10.
2. Victoria Nelson, "The Art of Memory," *The Threepenny Review* (issue 34, summer 1988), 3. PDF accessed at https://ur.booksc.eu/book/27435874/761d08.
3. Ibid.
4. As quoted in *Flower Power: A Studio-Visit Conversation between Paul Maziar & Srijon Chowdhury in Conjunction with Dandelion Song* (New York: AC Books and Foxy Production, 2021), 9.
5. Conversation with the author, November 18, 2021.
6. Conversation with the author, January 12, 2022.
7. Jo-Anne Birnie-Danzker, "The Apotheosis of Brutality: Franz von Stuck and America" in *Franz von Stuck* (Seattle: Frye Art Museum, 2013), 24.

The Family Romance of Srijon Chowdhury

1. Mónica Belevan, "Alamut, Bosch, Gaddis: Introduction to Epochal Art," *Covidian Aesthetics* (blog), December 10, 2020, https://covidianaesthetics.substack.com/p/alamut-bosch-gaddis-introduction. First published on *Ribbonfarm* (blog), April 28, 2020, https://www.ribbonfarm.com/?s=bosch.

The Miracle of Death: On the Work of Srijon Chowdhury

1. Theodor W. Adorno (1903–1969) was a leading figure in the Frankfurt School of critical theory. While his philosophical interests and influences are wide ranging, questions about art and aesthetics sit central to his thought. The notion that every work of art is the nexus of a problem is emphasized in the draft introduction to his *Aesthetic Theory*, which he was in the final stages of completing at the time of his death (and which was published in 1970). *Aesthetic Theory* represents a mature statement of Adorno's reflections on art, including complex analyses of art's history, relation to theory, and (most notable in the current context) function in society. For Adorno, works of art were singular expressions of the tensions and contradictions inherent in the everyday life of the contemporary world. Artworks, in his view, take us beyond the world (by providing for us the means to imagine how the world might be different) and yet refocus our position within the world (because every work of art is created according to the conditions of the world itself). This tension—between going beyond the world and situating us within the world—stands as a problem within each work of art. Yet for Adorno, it is precisely in this tension that one can find the kernel of truth that works of art have the power to reveal.
2. Gottfried Wilhelm Leibniz (1646–1716) was a polymath, working in (among other things) philosophy, mathematics, and science. In many ways, his thought can be understood as bridging the gap between early modern thinkers (like René Descartes and Nicolas Malebranche) and later thinkers (Christian Wolff and Immanuel Kant), all of whom influenced the history of philosophy that followed in their wake. Though Leibniz is certainly not the only thinker who represents a Late Baroque frame of thought, his work provides a key insight to the precision and decadence (a precision *with* decadence, as well as a decadence *with* precision) characteristic of the age.
3. Despite meeting an early death at age twenty-eight, Novalis (Georg Philipp Friedrich Freiherr von Hardenberg [1772–1801]) was an influential figure in the movement of Early German Romanticism. Novalis appreciated the fragmented nature of experience but envisioned a fundamental unity between all that existed. Such unity, he imagined, could be contemplated thanks to our aesthetic, poetic capacities. With these capacities we could *romanticize* the world. That is, we could begin to see the infinite in the finite, the spiritual in the material, and the mysterious in the mundane (and vice versa). It is within this frame of thought that Novalis was able to perceive not just life, but also death, in a new light, as something extraordinary and even magical. Novalis, *Notes for a Romantic Encyclopaedia*, trans. David W. Wood (New York: SUNY Press, 2007), 42.

Artist Biography and Exhibition History

Born in Dhaka, Bangladesh, in 1987
Lives and works in Portland, OR

Selected Solo Exhibitions and Two-Person Exhibitions

2022 *Srijon Chowdhury: Same Old Song*, Frye Art Museum, Seattle
Srijon Chowdhury: Groundhog Day, SE Cooper Contemporary, Portland, OR

2021 *A Still Life*, Ciaccia Levi, Paris
Dandelion Song, Foxy Production, New York

2020 *Srijon Chowdhury*, Foxy Production, New York

2019 *A Divine Dance*, Anat Ebgi, Los Angeles
Revelation Theater, Conceptual Fine Arts Live, Milan
Condo New York (with Stephen Lichty), Foxy Production, New York

2018 *Before Dreams*, Antoine Levi, Paris
The Coldest Night, Upfor, Portland, OR
Endings (with Bobbi Woods), The Art Gym, Marylhurst, OR

2016 *Memory Theater*, Upfor, Portland, OR
Since The Garden, Klowden Mann, Los Angeles

2014 *The Garden*, Klowden Mann, Los Angeles

2010 *Nepotism*, The Gallery, Dhaka, Bangladesh

Selected Group Exhibitions

2021 *Striving After Wind*, Chapter NY, New York

2020 *Severed Symbol*, Deli Gallery, Brooklyn
Barely Furtive Pleasures, Nir Altman, Munich

2019 *Cicatrices*, VO Curations, London
Portraits, Foxy Production, New York

2018 *Man-Thing versus Swamp Thing*, Et al., San Francisco

2017 *February*, Roberta Pelan, Toronto
Water & Dreams, The Green Gallery, Milwaukee
July Kamikazes: Blue, Pøst, Los Angeles
Ours Is a City of Writers, LAMAG, Los Angeles

2016 *Out of Sight*, Seattle
Imperceptibly and Slowly Opening, Vox Populi, Philadelphia

2015 *Imperceptibly and Slowly Opening*, Sector 2337, Chicago
The Great Debate About Art, Upfor, Portland, OR
Source Amnesia, Klowden Mann, Los Angeles
Sincerely Yours, Torrance Art Museum, Torrance, CA

2014 *The Beautiful Changes*, RH Contemporary Art, New York
Fictions, Klowden Mann, Los Angeles
Incognito, Santa Monica Museum of Art, Santa Monica
Not-Knowing, JAUS, Los Angeles

2013 *Walk the Line*, Launch Gallery, Los Angeles
Chess Set, Helen Bolsky Gallery, Los Angeles
LAndscape, Fredric Snitzer Gallery, Miami

Exhibition Checklist

All works by Srijon Chowdhury unless otherwise noted.

Pale Rider, 2019
Oil on canvas
84 × 192 in.
Collection of Lara and Jeff Sanderson

Mouth (Divine Dance), 2022
Oil on linen
Five panels, 126 × 72 in. each
Courtesy of Ciaccia Levi, Paris-Milan, and Foxy Production, New York

Ear (Good), 2022
Oil on linen
126 × 72 in.
Courtesy of Ciaccia Levi, Paris-Milan, and Foxy Production, New York

Ear (Bad), 2022
Oil on linen
126 × 72 in.
Courtesy of Ciaccia Levi, Paris-Milan, and Foxy Production, New York

Eye (Birth), 2022
Oil on linen
72 × 126 in.
Courtesy of Ciaccia Levi, Paris-Milan, and Foxy Production, New York

Eye (Morning Glory), 2022
Oil on linen
72 × 126 in.
Courtesy of Ciaccia Levi, Paris-Milan, and Foxy Production, New York

Nose (Crucifixion), 2022
Oil on linen
126 × 72 in.
Courtesy of Ciaccia Levi, Paris-Milan, and Foxy Production, New York

Sigil Gate, 2022
Welded steel
Six panels, 120 × 312 in. overall
Courtesy of Ciaccia Levi, Paris-Milan, and Foxy Production, New York

Franz von Stuck
German, 1863–1928
Die Sünde (Sin), ca. 1908
Tempera on canvas
34⅞ × 21⅝ in.
Frye Art Museum, Founding Collection, Gift of Charles and Emma Frye, 1952.169

Contributors

Mónica Belevan
Born in Lima, Mónica Belevan is a Peruvian writer, art historian, and entrepreneur. She is a co-founder and chief concept officer at Accursed Share, a crypto-art accelerator, and the editor-in-chief of *Covidian Aesthetics*. You can find her on Twitter: @LapsusLima.

SJ Cowan
SJ Cowan is a writer, philosopher, and artist. He currently lives in Berlin, Germany, where he is working with a research group in philosophy at the Free University. Additionally, he is pursuing a PhD in philosophy and critical theory at UC Berkeley. His dissertation project—which draws primarily on thinkers like Kant and Adorno—is on hope's relationship to aesthetic experience and art. He also holds degrees in theology and photography.

Amanda Donnan
Amanda Donnan is interim co-director and chief curator at the Frye Art Museum, where she has organized exhibitions ranging from the thematic survey *Group Therapy* (2018) to pairings such as *Dress Codes: Ellen Lesperance and Diane Simpson* (2019) and solo presentations including *Duane Linklater: mymothersside* (2021), *Agnieszka Polska: Love Bite* (2020), and *Tschabalala Self* (2019).

Frye Art Museum

Board of Trustees

Frye Art Museum Staff

This book is published in conjunction with the exhibition *Srijon Chowdhury: Same Old Song*, organized by the Frye Art Museum, Seattle, curated by Interim Co-Director and Chief Curator Amanda Donnan, and presented at the Frye, October 8, 2022–January 15, 2023.

The exhibition and publication are made possible with generous support from the Frye Foundation and Frye Members. Media sponsorship is provided by *The Stranger.*

FRYE
/Foundation

the Stranger

Library of Congress Cataloging-in-Publication Data

Names: Donnan, Amanda, editor. | Belevan, Mónica. | Cowan, SJ.
Title: Srijon Chowdhury : same old song / edited by Amanda Donnan.
Description: Seattle, WA : Frye Art Museum, [2022] | "This book is published in conjunction with the exhibition Srijon Chowdhury: Same Old Song, organized by the Frye Art Museum, Seattle, curated by Interim Co-Director and Chief Curator Amanda Donnan, and presented at the Frye, October 8, 2022–January 15, 2023"—Colophon.
Identifiers: LCCN 2022024216 | ISBN 9781646570300 (paperback)
Subjects: LCSH: Chowdhury, Srijon, 1987—Exhibitions.
Classification: LCC ND237.C4926 A4 2022 | DDC 759.13—dc23/eng/20220708
LC record available at https://lccn.loc.gov/2022024216

Designed by Purtill Family Business
Layout by Thomas Eykemans
Copyedited by Kathleen Garrett
Proofread by Janice Lee
Color separations by I/O Color, Seattle
Produced by Lucia|Marquand, Seattle
www.luciamarquand.com
Printed and bound by Artron Art Group, China

Cover: *Dandelion Song*, 2021. Oil on linen. 36 × 24 in. Private collection. Photo: Charles Benton

Back cover: *Making a painting*, 2016. Oil on linen. 60¼ × 48¼ in. Courtesy of Ciaccia Levi, Paris-Milan. Photo: Lee Thompson

Frye Art Museum
704 Terry Avenue
Seattle, WA 98104
USA
www.fryemuseum.org

Available through:
ARTBOOK | D.A.P.
75 Broad Street, Suite 630
New York, NY 10004
USA
www.artbook.com